TOGETHER IN AMERICA

The Story of Two Races and One Nation

TOGETHER

IN AMERICA

THE STORY OF TWO RACES
AND ONE NATION

Johanna Johnston

ILLUSTRATED BY MORT KÜNSTLER

DODD, MEAD & COMPANY
NEW YORK

Library of Congress Catalog Card Number: 65–13509

Apollo Edition

Printed in the United States of America

Author's Note

This book is not just about Negroes of achievement in America. It is not just about the special circumstances that have faced Negroes in this country for centuries. And although it scans America's past from the time of Columbus, it does not pretend to offer more than a very condensed outline of that history.

This book is simply an attempt to show that people of both European and African descent have contributed to America's discovery, growth and strength, from the beginning—that the contributions of some who labored under brutal disadvantages have been remarkable; and that the needs and pressures of the times have played a part in what happened and what was accomplished in every era.

Finally, this book carries the hope that one day the wrongs of the past (and present) need no longer shape our behavior toward each other, and that we will all recognize our mutual heritage as we live together more happily in the land we have shared so long.

JOHANNA JOHNSTON

New York City

Contents

TOGETHER IN AMERICA

The Story of Two Races and One Nation

Two Stories...

One story—a very familiar one—tells of all the men, and women too, who *chose* to come to America. That story most often begins with Columbus who, of course, did not know that it was a New World towards which he was sailing across the unknown Atlantic. Still, it was by his own choice that he embarked on such a daring voyage. And it was his own unswerving determination that kept his ships sailing on until he had found land to the westward, just as he had hoped.

Then, after Columbus, there came all the others, *choosing* the New World he had discovered, in spite of all its hardships and difficulties, because of various dreams they had. There were the Jamestown colonists, the Pilgrim Fathers, the Puritans, the settlers in the South, and then, finally, hosts and hosts of men and women from every country in Europe, coming to the New World because it seemed to promise them many things they could not find

1

in the countries where they had been born.

That familiar story is both thrilling and true as it tells of thousands coming to America because they had *chosen* it, and of all that they accomplished as they made it their home.

But that is not the whole story of America. There is another story that is a part of it and makes it even more wonderful. It is the story of men and women who did not come to the New World by choice at all, but were brought in chains, against their will.

Great areas of the New World were made to yield riches because of the labors of these men and women. Many things that were accomplished could not have been done without their help.

But the wonderful part is that even though they had not come by choice, almost from the beginning they gave their hearts to the new land in which they lived. Very soon they accepted America as home, just as the settlers did who had come in a far different fashion. The dreams of freedom that the New World inspired were theirs also. And from the beginning, they gave of their talents as well as their labor, whenever they were allowed to do so.

To list all the names and tell all the accomplishments of these people in this book is not possible. Here there is only an attempt to braid the story of those who came in chains to America into the more familiar story. And, by doing so, to make America's history even more wonderful as it becomes plain how *two* peoples carved a nation out of a wilderness—together.

1 *Explorers*
1450-1500

Light-skinned men from Europe, dark-skinned men from Africa—for centuries they had hardly known of each other's existence. They met with some surprise.

On an African beach, a white-robed man from Morocco, a Moor, stood watching as a curiously built ship anchored offshore. A small boat was lowered. A group of men rowed toward the beach. They landed, pulled up the boat, and looked about them.

The Moor recognized the men as Europeans and was surprised to see them here in Africa. Europeans had never sailed this far down the western coast of Africa before. He wondered what had brought them here.

He was even more surprised when the Europeans rushed across the beach and seized him as their captive. He cried out and protested in sign language. He tried to tell them that they did not want him. He was only a visitor in this territory, not a native. He gestured to them that they should follow him.

Walking beside the Moor suspiciously, the Europeans followed him inland till they came to a village of straw huts. Then they stared about them in wonder at the African men and women who quickly gathered. The Moor was talking with some man who seemed to be in authority, the chief of the village, perhaps. There were questions, answers, orders. Soon ten lively African boys were standing before the Europeans. It became plain that the Moor was offering the ten boys to the Europeans as captives in his place.

The Europeans stared at the boys and the boys stared back. And the Europeans considered the matter. Ten captives in place of one. Furthermore, it was unlikely that these boys were Moslems, as the Moor undoubtedly was. If the Europeans took the boys they could convert them to Christianity, as they would never be able to convert the Moor. Above all, there was the novelty of these handsome, healthy boys whose skins were darker than any the Europeans had ever seen.

The Europeans nodded, accepting the bargain. They marched the boys down to the beach, ordered them into the boat, and rowed them to the ship.

After some further voyaging down the coast, the ship turned back and returned to its home port in Portugal. The African boys were paraded through the streets of Lisbon. Everyone stared in wonder and delight at the strange young people. Rich men hurried to buy them as servants and houseboys. Those who were disappointed at not getting one hurried to put in orders for one or two with captains of ships that would soon be making the same voyage down the western coast of Africa.

It had all been an accident, really. The Moor had only been protecting his own freedom when he offered the boys in his place. The Portuguese captain who accepted them had not been planning to start a trade in such trophies. Like most of the other Portuguese captains of the time, he had been sailing in the waters off the western coast of Africa for quite another reason. Spurred on by Portugal's prince, Henry the Navigator, the captain had been trying to find his way to the southern tip of Africa. Prince Henry was urging all his captains to look for that tip, and a sea route around it, hoping it would lead Portuguese ships northward and eastward toward the Orient. The Orient was the goal—the land where spices grew, a land of gold and precious gems and silks and brocades.

But who could resist good trading if that was offered

along the way? The nuts, the fruits, the olive oil, the gold that Portuguese captains found in Africa, were all welcomed in Portugal. And the clever, handsome African boys and girls they began bringing back grew more and more popular.

No one in Portugal needed or wanted these Africans for hard labor. Negroes were exotic foreigners, more than anything else. Rich men liked to have them around as a sign of their wealth.

Before many years had passed, seven or eight hundred Africans a year were being brought to Portugal. And by the time one Portuguese sea captain did find his way around the southern tip of Africa, there were Negroes in Spain as well as Portugal. By then, not all of them were house servants either. Chances of fortune, loss of their masters, their own intelligence and ambition had led some of them into more independent careers. The color of their skin was different from that of the Europeans, but no one thought that meant they were born to be servants and nothing more. Some had little farms or businesses. Some became soldiers, sailors or pilots.

And so, soon enough, men from Europe and men from Africa were both part of the continuing push into unknown seas, as the search went on for a sea route to the Orient.

The Italian, Christopher Columbus, outfitting three small ships to sail westward on an expedition financed by Spain, hired a pilot named Pedro Alonso Niño. But his shipmates called the pilot *El Negro*.

El Negro shared the relief and joy of all Columbus' men when the little ships finally did find land after sailing westward across the terrifying Atlantic. He was with the treasure hunters landing on the islands, trying to find out from the natives if there was gold anywhere about. He tasted the strange food the natives were offering— pineapple, sugar cane, sweet peppers. And after the return to Spain, he was part of the triumphal parade from the seacoast to Barcelona, as Columbus made his way to King Ferdinand and Queen Isabella with proof of his wonderful discoveries—parrots, monkeys, coconuts, and plates of gold and silver.

El Negro sailed again with Columbus when Columbus made his third voyage to the islands, still looking for a channel through them that would lead to the mainland of China or India. Later, El Negro sailed with another ship that did touch on a mainland. It was the continent that would one day be known as South America. Like all the other treasure seekers hurrying across the Atlantic in Columbus' path, El Negro was baffled by not finding any of the spices, gems, silks, and other products men expected to find in the Orient. But he saw enough things of value to make him want to try a trading trip to this mainland coast.

Back home in Spain, El Negro won permission from the king to undertake such a voyage. He and a partner fitted out a ship, filled it with various European products, and set forth. Their voyage went well. Their trading went well. They returned to Spain with their hold full of rich and varied goods from South America. They had accomplished the first successful voyage across the Atlantic to be made for purely commercial reasons.

But El Negro was dead, and Columbus was dead too, when the greatest surprise of all began to dawn on the treasure seekers, and the men back home in Europe also. This was not some part of the Orient to which Columbus had led the way. These were islands, and a mainland, not marked on any map. They were unknown to any previous travelers, even those in the time of the ancient Greeks and Romans.

This was a New World.

It was a long time before a few observant men began to wonder if some Africans had found the New World years and years earlier. Men and women who looked very like Africans were living in South America when the men from Europe landed there. Some of the words they used—*yam, tobacco, canoe*—were African words, part of the native language when the Europeans arrived. Africans *could* have sailed their swift, light warships across the Atlantic to the South American shores, and then settled there.

But no one had time to speculate on such matters when the first surprise of a New World dawned. From all over Spain, daring, ambitious, hopeful soldiers-of-fortune rushed to the seaports to board ships for the New World, to explore, to conquer, and to find—who knew what treasure?

Africans were among them, as a matter of course. Some were servants of the Spaniards. Some were soldiers-of-fortune themselves.

African soldiers were part of Hernando Cortez' small army when he invaded Mexico and marched northward toward the Aztec cities in the interior. Like all the others, they marveled at the temples, the gardens, the lagoons of Montezuma's city high on the Mexican plateau. With the others, they helped to loot the wealth of the city for Spain.

But Cortez and his soldiers brought things to Mexico also. They brought the Christian religion. They brought an animal hitherto unknown in the New World—the horse.

And it was a Negro soldier in the army of Cortez who found a few grains of wheat in his rice rations one day and decided to plant them. According to legend, this unknown soldier then tended and reaped the first crop of wheat to be grown in the New World.

Thirty Africans were with Vasco Núñez de Balboa when he built his rude fleet of ships to sail along the Isthmus of Panama. They helped him hack his way across the jungle at the narrow part of that Isthmus. They were among the Spaniards and Indians with him when he first gazed on a vast new ocean, the Pacific.

Francisco Pizarro counted Negroes among the soldiers

in his small army of a hundred men, when he marched that army up into the Andes of South America, to outwit and conquer the army of the Incas. Later, after his conquest, when he was assassinated by conspirators among his own men, two loyal Negro soldiers carried Pizarro's body to the cathedral that had been built in the Incan city where he died, and they helped to bury him there.

Spanish leaders and officials were the ones who wrote the histories and reports of the expeditions. Naturally, they tended to write most about their own achievements and to ignore others without whose help they might not have done so well.

But one Spaniard's story of his long ordeal in the New World could not help but also be the story of the three men who shared it with him. Cabeza de Vaca had been a member of a large expedition that set out from Spain to invade and conquer Florida. But when the Spaniards landed on the Florida coast, the Indians attacked furiously. Many of the Spaniards were killed. All but one of their ships were destroyed. The survivors sailed away down the coast in the remaining ship. Then a storm blew up and wrecked that ship. Only four men managed to swim safely to the Florida shore—Cabeza de Vaca, two other Spaniards, and a Negro servant, Estevan, often called Estevanico, or "Little Stephen."

The four men had only one hope when they found themselves alive on the desolate coast. That was to try to make their way northward, up and around the Gulf of Mexico, and thence into Mexico and to the capital city where Cortez had established Spanish government.

They struggled through the Florida undergrowth, trying to sustain themselves on the strange vegetation. They were captured by Indians, who prepared to kill them. One of the Spaniards noticed an Indian lying ill. The Spaniard had a slight knowledge of medicine. He pretended that it was a knowledge of magic. He rattled a hollow gourd, and then with more signs of mystery, treated the sick Indian. Fortunately, the Indian began to get better. The captured Spaniards and the Negro, Estevan, were reprieved from the death sentence. Instead, the Indians put them to work as slaves.

The four men labored for the Indians day after day, plotting their escape. Finally, one night, they managed to get away safely. They struggled on through the wilderness. Again they were captured. Again, a show of magic and some medical treatment of a sick Indian saved them. Again, they were held as captives. Finally, they escaped these captors also.

Their ordeal went on and on. Still the four men struggled northward and westward toward their goal.

Eight long years after their shipwreck they arrived in Mexico City. The three Spaniards, exhausted, were glad to sail for Spain as soon as possible. But Estevan stayed on in Mexico City.

A few years later, in 1539, Cortez decided to send an expedition northward to look for a rich group of cities

which the Indians called the Seven Cities of Cibola. He
appointed a priest, Fray de Niza, to lead the expedition.
But he had heard of Estevan's amazing journey from
Florida to Mexico, and so he asked the Negro to go with
the party as a guide.

Estevan wore belled bracelets on his arms and ankles.
He carried the hollow gourd which had been so helpful
on the trip before. And he traveled in style and splendor
at the head of the expedition.

As the party traveled northward, the going grew more
and more difficult. At last de Niza decided to send Estevan, with a force of three hundred men, to scout out the
land ahead. He told Estevan to make a cross out of two
pieces of wood each night, and send it back to the waiting forces by a runner. A small cross would mean that all
was well but nothing of importance had been discovered.
Larger crosses would indicate that the trail was promising.

Day after day, Estevan and his men marched northward, and each night Estevan sent back a small cross.
Then one day he stopped in excitement and ordered a
cross as tall as a man to be constructed and hurried back
to de Niza.

Ahead, he saw what looked like a great walled city.

The runners left for the south with the large cross.
But Estevan was too eager to wait for the force in the
rear to join him. He decided to demand the surrender of
the city before him, and then, if that were not given at
once, to march on it and take it by force.

Such bold gestures had been successful before. But the men in the walled city refused to surrender. They gathered their forces swiftly. As Estevan and his men marched forward, they swept out onto the plain and fell upon their attackers. Estevan was killed. All but three of his men were killed. The three survivors fled back across the plain to warn de Niza and the army.

Frightened by this news, de Niza marched northward only far enough to see the walled city in the distance. Then he turned around and went back to Mexico City to report its discovery.

But Estevan was the first man from across the sea to find his way to that strange, walled city. It was not one of the Seven Cities of Cibola. Those remained a myth, like the Fountain of Youth that Ponce de Leon looked for in Florida. What Estevan had found was one of the great pueblo cities of the Zuñi Indians, in New Mexico.

Men from Europe, men from Africa—they had only really discovered each other's existence a hundred years before. But together they had joined in the discovery and conquest of a New World—a world that seemed to offer unlimited opportunities and rewards to them both.

2 *Planters on the Islands*
1500-1600

All over the islands—those lush and lovely islands that men now called the West Indies—something unexpected was happening.

The Spaniards who had settled there had taken it for granted that the native Indians would provide the labor force they needed. The Indians were all around—Indians whom they had fought and conquered. The Spaniards thought that they needed only to round up those natives and set them to work, and they would begin harvesting the riches of the mines and the fields.

But the Indians, who looked healthy enough, were proving strangely delicate. They had been used to easy, careless lives in their island paradises. They knew nothing about the discipline of agriculture. They were not used to long hours of effort in the mines.

And all over the islands, the Indians who were set to work by the Spaniards were dying.

The Spaniards grew desperate. They had to have workers. There was money to be made from the sugar cane, the pineapple, the peppers, the fruit—above all, from the tobacco that grew under the warm, tropical sun. But they had to have workers to plow and plant and tend the crops. There was money in the gold and silver mines. But they had to have workers to dig out the precious ore and carry it to the coast and load it on ships.

They made expeditions into the interiors of the islands, to round up more natives. They brought these natives back to the mines and plantations and set them to work. And these natives died too.

By the time the Spaniards had been living on Haiti for fifteen years, half of the island's population had died. It seemed quite likely that soon there would be no Indians left at all.

It was just then that the Spaniards began to look with new eyes on the Negro servants and slaves they had brought with them from Spain. The Negroes working in the fields did not faint and collapse as the Indians did.

The Negroes working in the mines had much more endurance than the Indians. What was more, the Negroes seemed to understand the principles of farming. The Spaniards knew little enough about Africa, the land from which the Negroes came. They did not know that many of the men of Africa had a long heritage of farming in their native land, and a long heritage of government and authority which helped them to work well with others.

What the Spaniards did remember now was that the Negroes among them, or at any rate their fathers or grandfathers, had been bought in Africa and brought to Portugal or Spain as *slaves*.

It was 1517 when a Spanish Bishop in Haiti, Bartolomé de Las Casas, wrote to Spain that he thought Negroes might solve the labor problem in the islands, and urging that as many Negroes as possible be sent there at once. Other planters and officials began writing the same kind of letters.

Soon ships were arriving from Spain with Negroes aboard, and the planters were hurrying to buy them. Then, as word about the planters' need spread among Portuguese and Spanish merchant captains, ships began arriving directly from Africa, their cargoes consisting of nothing but Negroes. A hundred, two hundred, five hundred, then a thousand and two thousand Africans were unloaded at the island ports. And the Spaniards were still hurrying to buy them and asking for more.

Soon the Spanish settlers were breathing sighs of relief. The Africans *were* much stronger than the Indians.

They did understand farming. They knew how to work, and could work, day after day, without collapsing.

Of course some fell ill and died. As the Spaniards grew more and more greedy to get every ounce of effort out of every field worker, many died. Many Africans rebelled against the hard labor and the cruel way they were treated, and tried to run away. A few succeeded, but most were killed when they attempted it. Soon there was a rapidly rising death rate among the Africans.

But now the Spaniards hardly bothered about how many workers died. The number of Africans whom they could get did not seem limited, as the number of Indians had been. Every month, the slave ships brought more—and more.

How was it possible? How was it that the Spaniards had only to ask, and thousands of Africans could be forcibly removed from their own country and taken to the islands?

At other times in history, whole peoples had been captured and forced from their own country to another. The Jews had been in slavery in Egypt for generations. Caesar had brought back Gauls and Britons to be slaves in Rome. But always those captives had been taken as slaves by an invading and conquering army. And no army was sent to Africa to take its people captive.

As it happened, no army was needed to conquer the people of Africa at this time. Two hundred years before, the story might have been different. Strong governments had united many small African tribes into nations then. But a series of weak kings had allowed those nations to fall apart again into small tribes. The tribes spent much of their time warring on each other, and taking captives from each other as tokens of victory. The chieftains had little use for these prisoners of war once they were captured. They were pleased to trade them to any interested Europeans for guns or whiskey or beads or blankets.

Spanish and Portuguese merchants had only to cruise along the West African coast, put in here and there and let their wants be known. There would generally be some chieftain, anxious to trade prisoners. If there was not, the merchants had only to hire kidnapping parties to go capture some Africans for them.

A reign of lawlessness was beginning in Africa, with the European merchants appealing to all the most greedy, vicious men in the country to capture fellow-Africans for them.

Of course, many of the people captured in this way resisted violently as they were being dragged and driven to the ships. They fought their African captors and their European captors. Many were killed. Many, hopeless and desperate after they were boarded on the ships, jumped overboard to their deaths. Many simply died in their wretched, huddled quarters aboard the ships.

But the merchants and slave traders cared as little about these captives who died on the way as the planters cared about the workers who died in the fields. Even if half their load of human beings died, the slave traders would still realize a profit on their cargo when they arrived in the islands. Then they could go back to Africa and get more.

The slave traders were growing wealthy dealing in this sort of merchandise.

And the planters on the islands were growing wealthy too.

History books tell of the exploits of the men who were hungry to win some of this wealth for themselves. England's John Hawkins became rich and famous by daring to sail his ships along the West African coast, into waters claimed by the Portuguese, to pick up Africans there and sail them to the West Indies. His nephew, Francis Drake, made a career out of pirate raids on Spanish ports and ships.

The Dutch were jealous of Spanish and Portuguese wealth also, and some of their captains edged into the slave trade. Others sailed among the islands of the West Indies looking for unclaimed ones they might seize for their country.

Wealth! The idea of it rose like a steamy perfume from the islands clustered in the round basin of the Caribbean, between the two American continents. And the desire for it helped trigger a war between England and Spain. The history books tell a good deal about the English sea dogs who vanquished the Spanish Armada, and so won for

England a new freedom of the seas—and a new freedom to engage in the slave trade.

But the histories have little to say about the slaves themselves—those thousands of Africans toiling in the West Indies on whose labor all this wealth was founded.

Men from Europe, men from Africa—they were still together in the New World. In fact, there were now many *more* Africans than Europeans in the islands. But there would no longer be opportunities for any of these Africans to stand out as individuals for a hundred years and more, except as the desperate ones rose in rebellion— and were quickly hunted down and killed. They would simply be members of a great, faceless mass, toiling hopelessly all their lives long. And the Europeans, except for their efforts to keep the Africans toiling that way, would try almost to forget their existence.

3 *Settlers on the Mainland*
1600-1661

Everything started off quite differently on the mainland of North America, northward from the West Indies. The English claimed much of this territory because of John Cabot's voyages of exploration down the North American coast. But the English were slow in trying to establish colonies. The first settlers, on an island off North Carolina, either died, were killed, or gave up in despair. Then, in 1608, a small group of Englishmen settled on an island at the mouth of the river they called the James, in the Virginia territory.

Eleven years later, those Englishmen in Jamestown, and others who had joined them, stared in wonder one day at twenty dazed, shackled, terrified Negroes. The Negroes had just been rowed ashore from a Dutch ship that had been blown off course on its way to the West Indies. The captain was offering them for sale in exchange for fresh water and supplies for his ship. But the English seemed bewildered at the idea of *buying* men and women as slaves.

It might have seemed that they would welcome slaves to help them. The eleven years at Jamestown had been hard ones, and nothing promised that the future would be much easier. The original colonists had wasted a year and more in a search for gold and had almost destroyed themselves and the colony by their single-minded goal. Then, saved by the energies of Captain John Smith, they had realized that the dream of gold was a mirage in Virginia, and that their one hope was to build farms in the wilderness by brutal, backbreaking work.

But slavery had not existed in England for centuries. The English had worked out another system for obtaining cheap labor. Poor men and women hired out their services to one master for a number of years, after which time they would have earned their freedom. This was called indenture. And in the eleven years of the colony's life, quite a few indentured servants had been brought over from England to help the colonists in their struggles with the wilderness.

Now, as the colonists stared at the Africans before

them, and as the Dutch captain urged and argued, that time-honored system of indenture was all the Englishmen could think of. They agreed to supply the Dutch ship with water and food, and to accept the twenty Africans as indentured servants in exchange.

There was a flurry of activity as kegs were filled with water, as grain, vegetables and haunches of smoked meat were collected. The boat was loaded and rowed out to the Dutch ship. Sails were hoisted, and the ship sailed away. The Englishmen turned their attention to the twenty new helpers they had acquired.

The Africans were half-naked, covered with the filth of the ship's hold, and they knew no words of the Englishmen's language. The colonists led them off to their rough huts, gave them water in which to wash, gave them food, rude clothing, places where they could sleep.

Then, somewhat restored, the African men were led by sign language to the fields, to the new buildings under construction, and offered hoes or spades or hammers. They picked up the tools and used them for the tasks at hand. The African women, dressed in strange, European dresses, were shown hearths, kettles, bowls for grinding meal, and they too, understood quickly enough what work was expected of them.

And so it was that a group of Africans came to that part of the New World that would one day be the United States, two years before the Pilgrims landed on the Mas-

sachusetts shore. When the Pilgrims began their struggle
with the wilderness, these Negroes had already become
well-acquainted with it. And by the time the Pilgrims
were celebrating a year's survival with a feast of Thanks-
giving, the Negroes of Virginia could have celebrated
three years of survival. They had done more than survive.
They had learned a new, strange language, and new customs and ways of doing things.

The Pilgrims brought their own religion with them to
give them strength and to regulate their lives. The Negroes of Virginia had to give up and forget the gods they
had known in Africa. Instead, they were introduced to
the religion of the Europeans and urged to make that
their own. And with surprising quickness and understanding, many of them grasped the basic teaching of
that new religion and found in it comfort and courage.

In due time, the period of indenture for the Jamestown
Negroes was over. They were free. Their labor belonged
to no man. Some were content to go on as they had been,
working for the same colonists they had served from the
beginning, but getting wages. Others had learned the
ways of the New World so well, they were able to take
up land of their own. They cleared wilderness for themselves and built small, rough houses. They planted crops,
gathered harvests, and some became so successful that
they, in their turn, were able to hire laborers to work for
them.

They had not come by choice to this New World, but

through their own efforts they had become part of it. The fields, the trees, the rivers and streams were theirs, as surely as they were those of the European colonists. Dark and white—they were all Virginians.

By this time, the rush of settlers to the mainland of North America had quickened. Few men who came were treasure seekers, as the Spaniards had been who hurried to the islands, to Mexico, and South America. The men of Europe—and the women too—who traveled across the ocean now saw another kind of promise in the vast, ungoverned lands of North America.

It was a place to establish settlements where they could worship exactly as they pleased . . .

A place where English Puritans could follow their religious ideas with no interference from the English Protestants . . .

A place where English Roman Catholics would also be free from persecution by those same Protestants . . .

A place where French Huguenots, or Protestants, would be free of persecution by French Roman Catholics . . .

And it was also a place where people who had known other kinds of misfortune in the Old World might find a chance to start again, a place where those who had had few opportunities might win lands and homes and better futures for themselves and their families.

So the new settlers came—from England, Scotland, Ireland and Germany and France. A good many came from Holland too, for the Dutch had their own claims in North America, along the river that Henry Hudson had found for them.

Poor men came, and men of substance, and men who called themselves gentlemen. Dreamers and fighters, ministers and scholars, and men who knew nothing of books but whose strong backs and arms were more helpful to them in the wilderness than any book learning.

Through these years, a few more Negroes arrived also. By now, there were colonists who were not at all bewildered by the idea of buying them as slaves. The Dutch, long since involved in the slave trade in the West Indies, brought Africans as slaves to help them cultivate their farms in the Hudson valley. And in 1638, a New England sea captain coming into Boston harbor from a voyage to the Indies, brought a cargo of cotton, tobacco—and Negroes, whom he had no difficulty in selling. The Puritans, deeply concerned about their own religion, seemed to see nothing wrong in buying and selling men and women who were outside the saving protection of their faith.

But still, for almost forty years, the European colonists made no effort to import Africans by the hundreds, as the men of the islands had done and were still doing. It was not that they did not have a labor problem. North and south, men needed help. In the northern colonies, where land was rocky, hilly and wooded, farms were limited in size and farm help was not needed so badly. But the colonists needed laborers in the seaports—men to help build ships, to help load and unload them, and to haul and carry.

In the southern colonies, where the sun was hot, and the land was wide and rolling, men had learned that some of the same crops that grew well in the islands flourished there—tobacco, indigo, sugar cane. Big plantations were already the rule, and the men who owned them needed field workers just as the planters in the West Indies did.

But still, men tried to solve the problem by asking for more and more indentured servants from England or elsewhere in Europe. Then they wrote also suggesting that men in jail for minor offenses be released and sent to the New World as servants, that beggars in the cities be rounded up, that young people without prospects be urged to come to America.

Many such miserable, hopeless and sometimes criminal characters were sent. But the wide, wild country of America lured many of them to run away from their masters long before their contracts were finished. It was almost impossible to trace them, once they had disappeared into the wilderness.

Gradually, the colonists began to realize that the darker skin of the Africans was very helpful, so far as this problem was concerned. Negro servants were much easier to trace when they ran away. When they suddenly appeared in a strange community, white men generally asked questions.

It was 1661, when the men in the Virginia colony put aside all the scruples that had restrained the Jamestown colonists forty years before, and decided to authorize Negro slavery by law. From now on when a man bought a Negro servant, he would be buying his services for *life*. A Negro was a slave, simply because he was a Negro.

No one seemed to realize that a brand-new idea was being added to the history of slavery—the idea that a man's race or *color* might doom him to slavery with no further argument about it.

In centuries past, in Greece and in Rome, dark men and white men had both been slaves. And according to their abilities, dark men and white men alike had served as teachers or preachers, and many were often honored as intellectuals or artists. An Ethiopian named Aesop, held as a slave in Greece, became the most famous story-teller of his time, and the tales he told endured through the ages.

Centuries later, a Spanish soldier named Miguel de Cervantes, was captured by the Barbary pirates, and he too became a slave, owned by a Moorish sultan. Later, after he had escaped back to Spain, he wrote a novel that became one of the world's classics. And it was at just about the same time as Cervantes was serving the sultan, that Captain John Smith, later to become the savior of the Jamestown colony, was captured and held as a slave by the Turks. Not even the Turks, who hated the Christian Europeans, suggested that John Smith's race or *skin color* made him their inferior. He was a Christian who had been captured by the fortunes of war. He escaped through his own daring, and that was that.

But the men of Virginia were tired of workers running away and vanishing without a trace. They needed workers they could keep track of, and from whom they could demand service all their lives long. So they wrote into law this new idea that a man's skin color made him a slave. Gradually, as the years went by, they would expand this idea, making the slavery of Negroes hereditary. And as they did this they would also begin justifying themselves by believing that Negro blood not only doomed a person to slavery but made him worthy of no better fate.

And up and down the North American seaboard, almost as though what the Virginians had done was a signal, the other colonies began writing the same kinds of laws authorizing Negro slavery into their statute books.

New colonies were being established, north and south —the Carolina colony, the Georgia colony, New Jersey, and William Penn's colony for Quakers in Pennsylvania. In all of them, Negro slavery was taken for granted almost from the beginning. Even William Penn, whose dream was a colony where men of all faiths might live together as brothers, felt that Negro servants were preferable to white ones, because they could be held for life. On the other hand, the sponsors of the Georgia colony tried to prohibit slavery in their first charter for that venture. But the settlers brought over from England to Georgia protested so violently that the sponsors had to take back the prohibition.

The slave-trading captains, already wealthy, hurried to take advantage of this brand-new market in North America. They crammed their ships with human beings in Africa and sailed to all the American colonies. Back and forth they voyaged, bringing Negroes by the hundreds, and then by the thousands.

Poor men, and men who had been people of substance in Africa—dreamers and fighters, priests and scholars, artists and athletes, men and women who had been princes and princesses, and some whose strong backs were their greatest assets—all these were pouring into America from Africa.

But with the new laws there, which reduced every man and woman of African blood to the status of a slave, it would be years before all these men and women of differing talents, backgrounds and intelligences, could begin to make themselves felt and known as individuals. That they were finally able to do it at all against the odds they faced was a triumph of their own endurance, energy —and oftentimes genius.

4 *Americans*
1661-1776

The land varied from colony to colony. The lives of the colonists varied. And their hopes—and their heroes—varied too.

The sternness of the land in New England seemed very much in keeping with the sternness of the religious faith that had brought settlers there. But the men working their farms, clearing the forests and building their little towns, accepted hardships uncomplainingly. Their hopes were centered on the heaven they were sure they would know after life's labors were over. And their earthly heroes were most often the ministers who preached the way to heaven—John Cotton, Richard Mather, and then the son and grandson of Richard, who became even more famous—Increase Mather and Cotton Mather.

But there were gentler souls as well in those northern colonies. America's first great poet, a woman, Anne Bradstreet, came to Massachusetts from England, and lived there till her death in 1672. One of her poems began:

> To sing of Wars, of Captains, and of Kings,
> Of Cities founded, Common-Wealths begun,
> For my mean pen are too superior things . . .

Still, Anne Bradstreet's delicate, lovely lyrics, "To My Dear and Loving Husband," "On the Burning of Our House," and others, start off every anthology of American verse.

There were teachers and educators too, founding schools so that everyone could learn to read the Bible, founding colleges to train ministers for the future. Harvard College was founded in 1636. The college in Connecticut that would one day become Yale University had also been established.

For the Negroes who were brought to New England, this respect for learning in the northern colonies was a fortunate thing. Quite a few of them were taught to read by their owners. In the towns and seaports, where Negroes often served as messengers and clerks, men also found it useful for them to read and write. And so, almost from the beginning, Negroes in the North had this advantage to help them understand and become part of the life in the New World, which was now, willy-nilly, their home.

The southern colonies, warm and sunshiny, wide and rolling, were a different world. The men there extended their holdings further and further. The most fortunate and energetic had plantations that covered thousands of acres, and they themselves were almost like feudal lords, ruling over vast domains.

They did not lack a hope of heaven, but they took far more joy in the pleasures of this life than the men in the North. They were proud of their homes, their hospitality, good food and wine and fine horses. They were proudest of all of being gentlemen.

Cultivated and worldly men, like William Berkeley, Royal Governor of Virginia, or Lord Calvert of Maryland, were southern heroes. There was also Nathaniel Bacon, leader of a revolt in Virginia, who has been honored as America's first rebel against English authority—but more likely he was simply a hot-headed young man seeking glory for himself.

Even the poor men of the South modeled their ways of thinking and behaving on the behavior of these gentlemen, dreaming of the day when they too would have more land, and slaves to tend it, and when they too would be proud, dashing elegant cavaliers.

For the Negroes whom fate brought to these southern

colonies, life was quite different from that known by the Negroes in the North. Their chief role was to provide the labor that made the big plantations possible. They were the peasantry, the less than peasantry, over whom the white gentry ruled.

There was no thought here in the South of teaching Negroes to read and write. In fact, doing so was generally forbidden by law. The white men felt it was not only unnecessary but actually dangerous for slaves to have such knowledge, for it might make them dissatisfied with their lots.

Some Negroes, more fortunate, were taught trades, or encouraged to use the skills they brought with them from Africa—blacksmithing, brickmaking, carpentering. Every big plantation was a village in itself, and these skills were valuable.

A few Negroes, the most fortunate slaves of all, were the ones who became house servants—cooks, valets and coachmen. Living in or near the gracious homes of their owners, they were the ones who found it easiest to learn the ways of the New World. Sometimes they had opportunities to learn to read. And they were the ones who often grew to feel loyalty and love to kind masters and mistresses.

And, of course, there were some free Negroes, descendents of the first African settlers in Virginia, and some who had been freed by the people who originally bought them. But most white men were not anxious to allow these free men many opportunities. Even in freedom, these men found their lives hedged about with many restrictions.

Still, even for the most unfortunate Negroes of the South, the field hands, the lands in which they labored grew less alien every day. They were not happy in slavery. They were overworked, often mistreated. But the land where they lived, its skies and hills and rivers, was beginning to be familiar and dear.

Land that varied—lives that varied. Northern and southern ways were combined in the middle colonies of New York, New Jersey and Pennsylvania. The small city of New York at the mouth of the Hudson was beginning to prosper as a seaport. Commerce and trade were thriving. Negroes there found a colony of busy, shrewd, impatient white men, who were inclined to treat them harshly, as marketable pieces of property.

But there was a kindlier life westward, in the rich fields of New Jersey and Pennsylvania. William Penn might have approved the lifetime slavery of Negroes, but the Quakers who followed him to Pennsylvania pondered a little longer. Many began to feel that slavery did not fit in with their belief in human brotherhood.

A group of Quakers first sent a petition to the legislature of their colony in 1688, protesting slavery and asking that it be prohibited. The legislature took no action, but many Quakers began legally freeing the Negroes they owned, anyway. They became even more concerned than the Puritans of New England with teaching Negroes to read and write. They set up schools for Negro children.

And there was still another kind of life along the frontier, which was forever creeping westward. The families that dared the howling wilderness which lay just beyond the towns and settlements knew nothing of the refinements men enjoyed in the towns of the South, nothing of the busy, religious routine that men followed in the towns of the North. They lived in rude cabins, fought Indians and wild beasts, and eked out scanty livings, farming and trapping.

Soon there would be thirteen colonies, edging the eastern seaboard of North America. But for a long time there would be no hint that some day a dream of freedom would unite the varied lives in all of them.

The Negroes in all the colonies, of course, had had a dream of freedom from the beginning. From the moment the first slave laws were passed, there had always been some trying to escape their bondage. And there had always been some who succeeded too, in spite of white men's hopes that they were marked men.

Some fled to the wilderness and joined their lives with those of the Indians. Some fled to the seacoast and shipped out with captains who needed men badly enough to ask no questions. And some, making their way to other colonies, were able to pass themselves off as free Negroes and build new lives.

The most desperate and daring of all plotted with their fellows, or with indentured white servants, or with the Indians, for organized revolts against their oppressors.

The names of those desperate men are not often recorded in history books. Their revolts were crushed. They were punished by death. No white men thought of them as heroes, daring everything for freedom.

The names that history does record in the 1730s and 1740s begin to be more and more familiar. Benjamin Franklin was making his way from Boston to Philadelphia to pursue the printing trade. He was founding a magazine, a literary club, and publishing an almanac that colonists everywhere relied on—*Poor Richard's Almanac.*

In tidewater Virginia, home of the gentlemen and cavaliers, George Washington was growing up, learning the surveyor's trade. Westward, in the rough country of the Virginia hills, young Thomas Jefferson was turning his inquiring intelligence on everything around him. And in the Massachusetts colony, young John Adams was applying his tough, independent mind to the law.

And then, in 1761, the name of a Negro appears. An individual was standing out, at last, from the vast, anonymous thousands of Negroes who had been in America so long and contributed so much labor to its development.

Jupiter Hammon was the man's name. He was a slave, but he was also a poet. His owners, who lived in Long Island, New York, were kindly people who had not tried to discourage his intelligence, but helped him to become educated. The years of Hammon's youth were years when a fever of religious enthusiasm was sweeping through all the colonies. Hammon was strongly moved by all the sermons he heard and the religious books he read. And then, his sensitive spirit responding to the beauty and drama of the Bible, he began to write poetry.

His owners were impressed and proud. They were so proud that they had some of Hammon's poems printed and distributed for sale in Hartford, Connecticut. Hartford was a literary center of the time, and long poems, printed on handbills, were often sold in the streets.

White men and women read, for the first time in 1761, the work of a Negro poet. And as they read "An Evening Thought. Salvation by Christ with Penitential Cries," they marveled that it had been written by a man whom they thought of as being a very different sort of person from themselves.

Then, only a few years later, they were hearing about, and reading, the verses of still another Negro poet.

A small, delicate girl had been kidnapped in the country of Senegal, in Africa, about the same time that Hammon's verses were first published. She had been flung onto a slave ship and brought to Boston. A Quaker, John Wheatley, saw her standing among the other captives on the wharf and felt a surge of pity for her frailty and youth. He bought her and took her home to his wife.

The Wheatleys named the child Phillis and gave her their own last name, and the Wheatley daughter began teaching her how to read. Phillis learned so quickly that within two years she was reading Latin classics as well as English books. By the time she was in her teens she was writing poetry.

Pleased and proud, just as Hammon's owners had been, the Wheatleys' first thought was to free this talented young person from the bonds of slavery, but Phillis continued to live with them as a daughter. Then they too arranged to have Phillis' poetry published.

Once again, everyone was astonished that a Negro should be able to write poetry. White men and women, even those most learned in Greek and Latin, were completely ignorant of the great tradition of poetry in Africa. They knew nothing of a wonderful poetic chronicle that had been written in Timbuctoo a hundred and fifty years before, nor of even earlier African poetry that was part of the heritage of that land.

They simply marveled at Phillis Wheatley's poetry as if at a miracle.

Worried about Phillis' health, which was still frail, the Wheatleys arranged a trip to England for her in 1773. The young poet knew even more fame and praise in England than she had known in the colonies. Lords and ladies befriended her. A book of her poems was published.

When she returned to America, there was a new hero in that country, George Washington. Phillis sent one of her poems to him and Washington responded kindly, inviting her to visit him. Later, she did so, and had a pleasant interview with him.

But soon after that, the older Wheatleys died, and Phillis began to know misfortune and unhappiness. She married a charming but ne'er-do-well sort of man who seemed unable to provide for her and the babies that were born to them. Phillis went to work in a boarding house to support herself and the children, and her frail health grew worse.

When Phillis died, in 1783, a very young woman, her poetry had been almost forgotten by the men and women of America. They had far different matters on their minds by then.

Freedom! The colonists had been so used to so much of it for so long that they were astonished when Parliament, in England, levied some taxes on all the colonies—taxes that were to help pay for the cost of their military defense.

In New England, men organized as Sons of Liberty and marched in the streets. Mobs, urged on by determined protesters like Samuel Adams, stormed the house of the British Governor in Massachusetts and set it afire.

In Virginia, a different world in so many ways, there was the same kind of reaction. Patrick Henry arose in the House of Burgesses to make a protest that echoed through all the colonies, likening George III to the tyrants of old, and crying, "If this be treason, make the most of it."

This kind of behavior in every colony had its effect in England. The Stamp Act was repealed. But then Parliament passed new laws, requiring other taxes from the colonies. And soldiers from England were stationed in Boston to oversee their collection.

Anger and resentment flared against the new taxes. And anger flared against the soldiers in Boston. People gathered along the waterfront where the soldiers were stationed, to show their displeasure by heckling the red-coated men.

Then, one evening, a group of British soldiers marched up the street with bayonets drawn. A crowd of sailors, deckhands and other waterfront workers collected at the end of the street and armed themselves with sticks and stones.

A tall man in the forefront of the crowd cried out, "The way to get rid of these soldiers is to attack the main guard." The sticks and stones began to fly.

In the confusion some British officer gave the order to fire. The tall man in the forefront was the first to fall. Then four others among the Americans fell.

As soon as the men went down, the British troops realized it had been a mistake to fire on them, and withdrew. The Bostonians gathered around to lift up the fallen, and to honor them in death as martyrs to the cause of liberty in America.

Bells tolled, church services and memorial meetings

were held. The event of that night of March 5, 1770, was soon being called the Boston Massacre. To many it signaled the real beginning of the American Revolution.

No one should have been too much surprised that the tall man who had fallen first was a man who had held a dream of freedom in his heart longer than most. Whether he had been born in Africa or America, no one knew. But he was a Negro. He had been a slave. He had run away and found a life of freedom for himself by becoming a sailor on a whaling ship. Then, ashore in Boston, he heard talk of threats to freedom that struck echoes in his heart that no white man could have known.

There had been different kinds of heroes in all the differing colonies. But the first to die in the cause that united them all was a Negro American—Crispus Attucks.

5 *Heroes of the Revolution*
1776-1783

They said "all"—the men gathered in Philadelphia in 1776 to spell out the principles for which the colonies were ready to fight. "We hold these truths to be self-evident: that all men are created equal . . . "

What each man really meant in his heart when he agreed to the word "all" would only be made clear later. But Thomas Jefferson wrote "all" in his draft of the Declaration of Independence. And the delegates to the Third Continental Congress went over his draft word by word. They deleted many things. They took out Jeffer-

43

son's long attack against the slave trade. They took out
the clause he had included that would prohibit the slave
trade in America in the future. But they left ". . . all men
are created equal."

Already, *all* kinds of people, from all the varying colonies, had begun fighting for the idea that every man was
born with an equal freedom to work out his own life
under laws which he had helped to make—and that,
somehow, was what the quarrel with England was all
about.

Already, Paul Revere, the silversmith, had ridden out
into the night to spread word about a force of British
soldiers on their way to Concord, to look for guns and
gunpowder that the colonists were supposed to have
stored there. Already, farmers and tradesmen, black-
smiths, millers, indentured servants and the masters who
hired them, had reached for their muskets, and gone out
to resist the British, and stop them in their march.

The backwoodsman, Ethan Allen, with his Green
Mountain Boys of Vermont, had stolen down to capture
Fort Ticonderoga on the banks of Lake Champlain, from
the British who held it. Among Allen's men had been a
Negro lad, Lemuel Haynes, who would go on to a fame
of his own after the war, becoming one of the best-known
Congregational ministers in Vermont, pastor to several
white congregations.

Already, before the Declaration of Independence was

signed, there had been fighting in Boston too. Farmers and tradesmen had fortified the heights of Bunker Hill. And Israel Putnam, commander of these untrained troops had cautioned his men to save their gunpowder till the last moment and rely on their marksmanship. "Don't fire until you see the whites of their eyes," he said.

There were Negro Americans among those stubborn defenders. One was Peter Salem, a man who had been held as a slave until just a few days before the battle, when his master legally freed him. Holding his musket ready, Salem watched the slopes below him. A British officer, rallying his men up the hill, jumped onto a redoubt and cried, "The day is ours." Salem fired. The officer, Major Pitcairn, fell. That British rally was halted.

Salem Poor was another hero. He fought so bravely that after the battle, his superiors recommended a citation for him. "We only beg leave to say," they wrote, "that in the person of this negro centres a brave and gallant soldier. The reward due to so great and distinguished a character, we submit to the Congress."

Not long after that, George Washington, newly appointed Commander-in-chief of the Continental Army, ordered that Negroes be banned from the army. Eager for as many soldiers as possible, he still ordered that Negroes already enlisted be discharged.

Washington feared only what many white men feared. They were afraid that if they gave guns to the Negroes whom they had enslaved, the Negroes would turn against them, and not against the British. It was a logical fear, perhaps, but it did not take into consideration the fact that thousands of Africans, just as thousands of Europeans, had grown to know America as a homeland. It was a land for which all its natives would fight, forgetting their quarrels with each other in the larger fight against a common enemy and for a common goal.

Protests against Washington's order banning Negroes from the army came from many Negroes. Among the first to ask him to reconsider was a young Bostonian named Prince Hall. He had been born in the West Indies, but had come to America as a youth and was soon a leader among Boston Negroes. After the war, he too would go on to fame among the Negroes of America as the founder of the Masonic Lodge for Negro Americans.

But no protests did any good.

Then, the British governor in Virginia, eager for troops to fight against the colonists, offered slaves their freedom if they would join the British forces. Some Virginia slaves, with personal freedom as their goal, joined the British army.

This British offer changed the minds of the colonists. Various military leaders in the colonies began recruiting Negroes into their regiments. Washington also took back his previous order and announced that free Negroes would thereafter be accepted in the Continental Army.

Was Washington surprised at how many responded to

even this reluctant invitation? Did he wonder at how many put loyalty to the land of their birth over their own grievances? History does not say. But it is on record that when Washington made his fateful crossing of the Delaware River on Christmas Eve in 1776, to steal up on the British-hired Hessians who were keeping holiday, two Negroes were in the boat with him. Their names are recorded: Prince Whipple and Oliver Cromwell. And since history says nothing more about them, it is logical to believe that they did their part, like all the others, in making his surprise successful.

History books tell of a few hard-won victories by the Continental forces, and of many discouraging defeats. They tell of how many volunteers, despairing of the colonial cause, left the army to return to their farms and shops.

But there were also those who refused to give up. And among them were several regiments of Negro volunteers that had been formed in Massachusetts, Rhode Island and Connecticut. One Massachusetts company that called itself the "Bucks of America" was led by a Negro commander. Another Massachusetts company had a white commander. Many Negroes were members of white regiments.

The loyalty and bravery of all these men did not go unnoticed at the time. After a battle in Rhode Island in

1778, the commander of the American forces requested a citation for a Negro regiment which had fought in the battle and "distinguished itself by deeds of desperate valor."

"All men are created equal . . ." Many men in Europe had been thrilled when the American colonists declared that was the principle for which they were fighting. It was the first time that people anywhere had dared put to the test the new idea that men had a "natural right" to freedom. A few Europeans—Baron von Steuben of Germany, Casimir Pulaski of Poland, Marquis de Lafayette of France, among them—were so excited that they crossed the ocean to help the colonists in their fight to win this "natural right."

That men of African ancestry as well as men of European descent were taking part in the fight seemed only logical to these Europeans. America was a homeland for both of them. And perhaps the visitors from Europe saw even more clearly than the colonists how valiantly Negro Americans fought for the great new ideal.

Lafayette had many words of praise for the Negro soldiers he saw in action. Later, he singled out one man for special mention. Gratefully, Lafayette said that James Armistead's scouting and reports had helped to save him and the forces under his command from capture by the British general, Charles Cornwallis.

And Armistead was only one of many Negroes who

served in the same dangerous role of spy and scout. One man, known only as Pompey, gathered the information that helped General Anthony Wayne to succeed in the battle at Stony Point in New York in 1779.

The Revolution had its sea heroes also, as the sailors of the Continental Navy harried and worried the ships of England. And Negro sailors were aboard many of the ships, helping in many capacities to achieve the victories that were won at sea.

John Paul Jones was a Revolutionary hero who has been enshrined in legend. His own ship, the *Bonhomme Richard,* about to sink beneath him, he called out defiance to the British ship which had nearly destroyed him. "I have not yet begun to fight," he cried. And wonderfully, he and his men did fight for four more hours, and took the British ship captive at the end.

A Negro lad of fourteen was a hero who is not so well-remembered. His name was James Forten. He was from Philadelphia, and he had enlisted as a powder boy aboard the *Royal Louis,* under the command of Stephen Decatur. Young James took part in many successful sea fights against the British. But then came a battle that ended in defeat. One of the English sailors took pity on the young lad, and offered to take him to his own home in England. James proudly refused the offer. He said that he felt he should suffer a prisoner's lot like all the other sailors on board the *Royal Louis.* To do less in the cause of independence would be to betray his country.

Legend tells of the women who helped in the American cause. There was Betsy Ross, and whether or not she really did make the first American flag, her name is part of America's folklore. So is that of Molly Pitcher, who won that nickname by carrying water to the fighters during the battle of Monmouth. Then, when her husband was killed before her eyes, she took his place behind a cannon and kept it firing until the battle was over.

Legend could also include another heroine, the Negro woman Deborah Gannet. Her eagerness to help the colonial cause was so great that she disguised herself as a man and served for a year and a half with a Massachusetts regiment.

Five thousand Negro Americans, all told, served in the Continental Army and Navy before the war was over.

Then, at last, after French troops and French ships had come across the ocean to add their strength to the colonial forces, the Americans began to triumph. In October, 1781, the British General Cornwallis, who had been besieged in Yorktown for seventeen days, surrendered his forces to General Washington. The rebellion had been successful.

It was time now to see how well the men of thirteen states, comprising a brand-new nation, could put into action and practice the great idea that all men were born with a "natural right" to "life, liberty and the pursuit of happiness."

6 *Free Men*
1783-1803

The air was full of a challenge to try new things, things
never attempted before. Men wanted to show the whole
world how much more they could accomplish in freedom
than when they were bound or restricted in any way.

Negro as well as white Americans felt the challenge—
for slavery was no longer the rule all over the land. Fighting a war for freedom had caused many people to realize
the injustice of some men holding others as slaves. Even
before the Revolution began, the men of Rhode Island
had decided that "those who are desirous of enjoying all

the advantages of liberty themselves should be willing to extend personal liberty to others." They had ruled that any Negroes brought into that colony should be free.

A slave in Massachusetts, Quock Walker, sued for his freedom, demanding it as a "natural right." The court ruled in his favor, and after that, slavery was ended in Massachusetts. Plans for a gradual ending of slavery had been made in Pennsylvania. Similar plans and laws were being worked out in all the northern states.

Many people in the southern states were wishing that they could follow in the same course. But it seemed to them that they had been trapped by circumstances so that they had to move more slowly than the men in the North.

The nature of the land in the South had meant that many, many more Negroes had been brought there as slaves than had been brought to the North. Most of these Negroes had been driven to the fields to work, and they had been forbidden to learn any of the skills that would enable them to be independent. As a result, many southerners who sincerely disapproved of slavery, wondered if it would be fair to the Negroes themselves to free them and cast them adrift in the world.

The nature of the land had created other problems. The big plantation owners really did not know how they could work their vast acres without slave labor. And for men who owned many slaves, there was a financial problem as well. They had paid a great deal of money for those workers, so that the slaves were an investment, like

land or livestock. Freeing their slaves would be the same
as throwing away money.

Still, a few southerners were flying in the face of cau-
tion and freeing their slaves anyway. And many, many
men were hoping that something would happen—they
were not sure what—that would make it possible for all
slavery to be ended in the South, some day.

Freedom was in the air, and a challenge to show what
could be done with freedom.

The Founding Fathers, fifty-five men in knee breeches,
buckled shoes and powdered wigs, were meeting the
challenge as it affected all the thirteen states of the new
nation. They were gathering to frame a Constitution that
would "establish justice, insure domestic tranquillity . . .
promote the general welfare."

At the same time, Negro Americans were blazing new
trails also.

Poets and patriots had been the first to emerge as individuals from the great blurred mass of men, women
and children held as slaves. Now there began to be
others, many others, responding to the new atmosphere
of freedom.

Benjamin Banneker was one of these, as truly a man of
the eighteenth century in the wide variety of his interests and accomplishments as those versatile leaders, Benjamin Franklin and Thomas Jefferson.

Born in Maryland, some years before the Revolution,

Benjamin Banneker was the son of a freed slave who worked his own small farm. He had made the most of every crumb of knowledge that came his way when he was a boy. A small school for Negro children had been nearby, and so he had learned to read and write. But once he had read all the books in the school, he had no way to get any more.

Growing up, he had no choice but to follow in his father's footsteps, working on the farm. But Banneker's mind was never idle. He tinkered with farm machinery and invented improvements for them. Then he invented and finally constructed an elaborate striking clock.

Some Quakers moved into the neighborhood, met the young man—and were amazed by the clock Banneker had made. It seemed likely to them that it was the first striking clock that had ever been manufactured in the colonies. One Quaker became especially interested in Banneker and began lending him books.

Banneker flung himself at this new opportunity, devouring the books. There was a book on surveying. He taught himself the trade and became an accomplished surveyor. There were books on mathematics and astronomy. He pored over those, studying the astronomical problems till he had become a competent astronomer. And he worked through the mathematical problems so carefully and exactly that he was even able to discover mistakes in the text.

Word about this unusual Negro mathematician and scholar began to spread. A celebrated doctor and scientist in Philadelphia, Dr. Benjamin Rush, heard about the accomplishments of Benjamin Banneker in Maryland. He found out more, and finally wrote to Thomas Jefferson about him. Jefferson, delighted by every advance of human intelligence, and every evidence that dark-skinned men were as talented and capable as white, became acquainted with Banneker himself. Then Jefferson recommended that Banneker be asked to join the group of men commissioned to survey and lay out the new capital city of the nation, Washington, D. C.

Banneker served with distinction on that important commission. Then he went on to still further proofs of his talent and originality. Along with his other activities, he wrote and published an almanac for several years, just as Benjamin Franklin had done for so long.

Negro Americans were becoming successful as business men. James Forten, the brave powder boy aboard the *Royal Louis* during the Revolution, went to work after the war and developed a new device to use in making sails for sailing ships. Soon he established his own sail loft in Philadelphia. He employed both white and Negro workers in the sail loft, and his business prospered.

Paul Cuffe was another who had made the most of every small opportunity. His home was in New Bedford, the whaling town in Massachusetts, and like many another New Bedford boy, Cuffe had shipped out on a whaler when he was just sixteen.

But that was only the beginning for Cuffe. Through hard work and intelligence, he advanced in rating. He became the captain of a whaling ship. Then, within a few years, he was able to buy a ship of his own. Misfortune struck when that ship was captured by pirates, but Cuffe refused to be discouraged. He managed to acquire another, better ship, and then, one by one, he bought others, till he was the owner of a small fleet. By this time, he also was the owner of a fair amount of land property as well.

A shipowner, a property owner, a taxpayer, Paul Cuffe began petitioning the Massachusetts legislature for the right to vote. This was a privilege restricted to white property owners, even in the northern states which had freed the Negroes.

But in this time of hope and accomplishment, it seemed that surely it was only a matter of time until the color of a man's skin would have no bearing on his rights as an American.

A Negro doctor emerged. James Derham had been a slave, owned first by a doctor in Philadelphia, then by a British army surgeon during the war, who sold him to a New Orleans physician after the war. All of the doctors had encouraged Derham's native abilities, training him to more and more responsibility as an assistant. Finally, his New Orleans owner helped Derham to buy his freedom, and James Derham went into medical practice in New Orleans for himself. New Orleans was an old French-Spanish city where there was less feeling that Negroes were born to be slaves than there was elsewhere in the South. Derham soon established a good practice and had a long, successful career.

The first book to tell the story of one man's experiences as a slave after being kidnapped in Africa was published —*The Interesting Narrative of the Life of Oloudah Equiano, or Gustavus Vassa*. Vassa had purchased his freedom and was living in England by the time he wrote the book, but his adventures had included some years as a slave to a Virginia planter, and then to a Philadelphia merchant. And the whole story was not only "interesting," as he called it, but dramatic, horrifying, inspiring, and a powerful argument against slavery.

Richard Allen and Absalom Jones of Philadelphia were two more Negro individuals beginning to stand out from the throng. Both had worked to buy their own freedom before the legal end of slavery in Pennsylvania. Both had become educated men through their own efforts. And both were well-known to Dr. Benjamin Rush, the Philadelphian who had encouraged Banneker. Dr. Rush had special reason for gratitude to Allen and Jones. In 1793, when a yellow fever epidemic struck Philadelphia, almost no white men would join the overworked doctor in his efforts to care for the sick and dying. But Richard Allen and Absalom Jones put aside their own fears of infection and worked beside him, day after day, till the epidemic was ended.

Dramatic things were happening even in the southern states. Many men there, looking at ignorant field hands to whom learning was forbidden, reasoned with a sort of upside-down logic that Negroes were mentally incapable of being educated.

One North Carolina man doubted that theory. In fact, he doubted it so completely that he wagered another man that a clever Negro youth could do as well in college as a clever white one. Enough people grew interested in the debate to put up the money to send one intelligent local boy, John Chavis, north to Princeton College.

The man who believed in Chavis won the wager. Chavis returned to North Carolina with such a fine education, such a poised and cultivated manner, that he was able to start a preparatory school for boys. He proved to be such an excellent teacher that soon many white boys were enrolled in his school—some of them the sons of the very men who had doubted that Negroes could profit by an education. Before many years, John Chavis' school became famous throughout the state of North Carolina.

A time of hope—and accomplishment!

Slavery still was the law in the southern states. The Founding Fathers, writing the Constitution, had yielded to the southern members who wanted their property rights in slaves protected. They had left the whole issue of slavery to the decision of the individual states. It was just one of many issues on which they had had to compromise, for fifty-five men had many points of view on many matters.

But with their compromises they had at last achieved a Constitution that all thirteen states had accepted—a Constitution that was actually *working*. It was a Constitution flexible enough in many ways so that it could be interpreted to fit men's changing needs and hopes. And so, as John Adams followed George Washington as President, there were many who felt that the silence of the Constitution in regard to slavery would not be a permanent thing. The need for slavery in the South would gradually be ended. The Negroes there would become more and more capable of freedom. Soon all Americans, whether they had come originally from Europe or from Africa, would be equal under the Constitution's law.

Then two things happened in the South.

The first was Eli Whitney's invention of the cotton gin —a simple but clever little engine that cleaned cotton seeds from the cotton bolls *mechanically*.

This invention did away with the tedious hand-cleaning of cotton and made cotton a profitable crop to grow in the South for the first time.

Quickly, men all over the South began making copies of Whitney's engine and selling them to landowners. Quickly, landowners set their slaves to work planting and tending acres and acres of cotton. Then, with dismay, they remembered that Congress had passed a law providing that the slave trade with Africa should end in 1808. Quickly they began buying more Negroes from the slave-trading ships so that they would have the help they needed to plant even more acres to cotton in the future.

Then the second thing happened. A plot for a massive revolt of slaves around Richmond, Virginia, was discovered.

A quiet, thoughtful young man, named Gabriel Prosser, had been the ringleader. He had pondered on all he had heard about liberty during the Revolution. He had heard about the Revolution in France too, when the poor rose against their aristocratic oppressors. Then had come news of the great and successful revolution of Negroes in Haiti, led by Toussaint L'Ouverture. At last, Prosser had become convinced that only a similar uprising in the South would free the Negroes there.

He had laid his plans carefully, and more than a thousand Negroes had rallied around him at a chosen spot outside Richmond on the night appointed by Prosser. They were making ready to march on the city when a cloudburst broke upon them. And that had been their undoing.

With roads and bridges washed out and the countryside a morass of mud, Prosser had decided to postpone the uprising. The slaves returned to their homes. And somehow, a hint of where they had been and what they were planning, came to the ears of their owners.

Prosser was seized at once. So were as many of his fellows as could be identified. There was no thought among the white men for Prosser's quiet dignity as he went to his death, refusing to name any of the others who had conspired with him. There was no feeling of sympathy for the desire for freedom that had inspired the plans for the uprising.

There was only horror that so many Negroes had been part of the plot, and a great fear that something like this could happen again, and next time the plot might not be discovered in time.

And so the white men of Virginia tightened all their rules and regulations regarding slaves, giving them less freedom to meet, to move around, to learn to read and write. For now, it was not just that white men feared for their personal safety if Negroes rebelled. They *needed* Negroes as slaves—needed them as never before—to plant and tend and harvest the crop that was going to make southern landowners rich—cotton.

By 1800, the great hope that slavery would gradually end in the South as it had already been ended in the North, had begun to fade.

But the dream, once glimpsed, would not vanish. The great idea that "all men are created equal" had taken root in the hearts and minds of men, both white and black, all over America. And wherever there was the slightest opportunity, in the South as well as the North, men of talent and energy would seize their opportunity, and continue to prove, through their achievements, the truth of the great idea.

7 *Pioneers*

1800-1820

The frontier, the wild land, the wilderness, always edging the settlements to the west, had offered a special kind of freedom to Americans from the beginning. Daniel Boone went hunting and trapping along the frontier in the days before the Revolution, charting the way for the settlements that would follow later. Davy Crockett, setting out from what had once been the frontier in Tennessee, traveled still farther westward.

Jean Baptiste Pointe De Sable was another adventurer in the wilderness, charting the way for others to follow.

He was not a rough, home-spun character like Daniel Boone or Crockett, but a handsome, well-educated young West Indian. He had been sailing his own ship from the islands to New Orleans in 1760, planning to settle in that city. Then his ship was wrecked in a storm. De Sable managed to get ashore with his life, but he had lost everything he owned, including all the papers which proved he was a free man. Even in New Orleans, a Negro without such papers was in constant danger of being stopped, held, and then sold as a slave.

No wilderness terrors could equal that danger, the young man felt. And so he soon slipped away from the city with two friends and started northward, following the Mississippi. Farther and farther north they went, into country untraveled since the days of LaSalle's voyage down the great river. Finally, in 1772, De Sable settled down and established a trading post near a river that the Indians called the Eschicagou. Like Boone and Crockett, and many another settler on the frontier, De Sable had chosen a spot well situated for further development. Some years later, a fort would be built where he had settled. And years and years later, the city of Chicago would rise on the site of his little trading post.

After 1803, when President Jefferson doubled the size of the United States with the lucky purchase of the Louisiana Territory from France, there was an even greater interest in moving into the western territories.

Families from Pennsylvania, New York and Virginia loaded furniture and tools on wagons and started out for Kentucky and Indiana. And men from the southern states of South Carolina and Georgia began moving westward too, into Alabama and Mississippi and Louisiana.

Cotton was beginning to make a great deal of money for southern planters, just as they had hoped it would. But cotton used up the richness of the soil very quickly. If the planters wanted their crops to flourish, they had to plant in fresh soil every few years. So they moved westward, with their families and their slaves, into rich bottom lands.

Indian troubles along the frontier, quarrels with the British who edged down from Canada into these western territories, began agitating the Americans in the West. Some of them, hot-headed and impatient, were sure that the English were conspiring with the Indians. This fear, along with the news of English insults to American ships at sea, made them eager to prove America's growing strength by another war with England.

The War of 1812 was not popular with all Americans. The merchants of New England did not like anything that interfered with their profitable trading voyages. And there were others who were reluctant to fight.

But once again, just as at the time of the Revolution, the Negroes of America were willing to forget their own grievances and fight for their homeland.

Fears of a British attack from the harbor were alarming the people of Philadelphia. The two Negro leaders, Richard Allen and Absalom Jones, who had helped their city during the yellow fever epidemic, again stepped forward. They rallied 2,000 Philadelphia Negroes to work for forty-eight hours without a break, building fortifications along the waterfront.

Negroes, Indians and frontier scouts were the only crew that the young naval officer, Oliver Hazard Perry, could find to man his makeshift fleet when he set out onto Lake Erie to track down the British ships cruising there. But his men made up in spirit what they lacked in naval training. After their miraculous victory, Perry's chief words of praise were for the dark-skinned Americans who had fought with him. It was due a great deal to their efforts that he had been able to send the famous message, "We have met the enemy and they are ours . . ."

General Andrew Jackson also had high praise for the Negro battalions that fought under his command at New Orleans. "I expected much of you," he told them after the battle, "but you surpass my hopes . . . Soldiers, the President of the United States shall be informed of your conduct on the present occasion; and the voice of the Representatives of the American nation shall applaud your valor, as your general now praises your ardor."

So why did so many northerners have such a curious change of attitude to the Negroes among them, after the war? Even in liberal Philadelphia, quiet, well-dressed, hard-working Negro Americans found their lives less pleasant. Work was harder to get, pay lower, their ordinary privileges were withdrawn or restricted.

What had happened? Were there some white people who felt threatened by what Negroes had shown they could accomplish, with even a small amount of encouragement and opportunity? Immigrants from Europe were coming to the United States in an ever-growing number. Were they fearful of competition for jobs they wanted for themselves?

Whatever it was, the bright years of hope for *all* Americans, including many who had been in the country far longer than the immigrants from Europe, seemed over.

The history books call the years of James Monroe's Presidency the Era of Good Feeling. For once, there was little conflict between different sections of the country. The southerners were growing rich on cotton, and in these years, their prosperity seemed to benefit northerners as well. And north, south and west, men were interested in developing the country as a whole, building roads and canals to link towns and markets and farms.

Everywhere, Negro Americans were helping with that building. But almost nowhere, north or south, were there many Negro Americans who would have called this an Era of Good Feeling.

Richard Allen and Absalom Jones were in church one

Sunday, their heads bowed in prayer. A group of white men and women of the congregation came to them and hauled them to their feet, telling them that in the future they could not worship with the white parishioners, but must sit in the balcony.

Jones and Allen swallowed their hurt and bewilderment. Quietly, they set about forming a separate branch of the Methodist Church in Philadelphia, for Negroes only. Before this time, whites and Negroes had generally worshipped together in churches of every denomination. After the church started by Allen and Jones, more and more separate churches for Negroes would be started, until finally people would begin to think that such separation had always been the custom.

Paul Cuffe, the whaling captain, had been noticing a new unfriendliness in the air even before the War of 1812. A despair had begun to grow in him. He wondered if the Negroes of America should just give up and go away from the country altogether. Africa had been the homeland of their fathers. Perhaps they should go to Africa and try to build new and better lives there. By 1811, a group of free Negroes had already decided on such a move. Cuffe sailed them to Africa in one of his ships. They landed on the western coast and planned to start a settlement. Returning to America, Cuffe wondered if he should not have stayed with them.

Other free Negroes took up the idea of emigrating to Africa. After the war, a veteran named Elijah Johnson sailed for Africa with a hundred free Negroes to help in establishing still another settlement there.

There were, of course, some white men and women, who took no part in this new unfriendliness to their fellow-Americans, just as there had always been some white people protesting slavery, protesting injustice and unfairness to Negroes.

Troubled by the continuing difficulties that faced Negro Americans, some of these white men and women began helping those who were interested in leaving America for Africa.

Soon they were joined in their efforts by quite a few slave owners who also approved the idea of Negroes emigrating to Africa. It was really not so odd for them to do so. *Free* Negroes were the only ones whom the slave owners wanted to send away. Slave owners looked on *free* Negroes, who could read and write and manage their own lives, as continual threats to the whole system of slavery. Free Negroes could encourage Negroes held as slaves to run away, or help them to buy their freedom. Just the sight of a free Negro could give a Negro held in slavery ideas of freedom for himself, ideas that freedom was possible.

A Colonization Society was organized, made up of men and women inspired by widely differing reasons. Some truly wanted to help Negro Americans. Some simply wanted to be rid of any who were free. But, joined together in what seemed like a worthy aim, they interested President Monroe in the colonization project. Soon the government had authorized the purchase of some miles of land along the coast of western Africa which was to become the new colony of Liberia. A capital city for the new colony was laid out and called Monrovia, after President Monroe. The society worked to gather funds to help Negro Americans emigrate to this new land of Liberia.

But how many Americans, whose forefathers had been kidnapped from that African homeland, were eager to be hurried back in the same direction, simply because some other Americans did not like the color of their skins?

Not so many.

James Forten, who had once refused freedom in England because he was willing to suffer for the cause of liberty in America, was one free Negro who was not. He spoke before a meeting of the African Methodist Episcopal Church in Philadelphia, and he urged all its members to join him in disapproving the idea of sending Negro Americans away from their homeland.

Paul Cuffe, after earnest thought, also turned against the African dream. He was an American first of all, whatever the hazards and difficulties. And he also realized that a few free Negroes leaving America would never help the thousands who would have to remain—in slavery.

There were others who voiced their unwillingness to

give up their homes in America and leave for a new land. Perhaps the most moving words of all were published by a convention of Negroes that met in Hartford, Connecticut.

"Why should we leave this land," they asked, "so dearly bought by the blood, groans and tears of our fathers? This is our home; here let us live and here let us die."

Still the Colonization Society continued its efforts through the next twenty years or so, helping a few thousand Negroes each year to emigrate to Liberia. Many of those who went did find rewarding lives in the new colony. But the total number who emigrated was very, very small in proportion to the number who stayed in America.

For those who remained in America—some because of their faith in it, and many because, as slaves, they knew nothing about the colony of Liberia—the years ahead would not be easy.

The movement toward the west was creating new states, north and south. Somehow, the balance between the states that allowed slavery and those that did not was kept even for a while. Then came the question of admitting Missouri as a slave state.

That question was settled—or seemed to be—by the Missouri Compromise. A line was drawn east and west across the whole continent. North of the line, slavery would be forever forbidden. South of it, slavery would be permitted.

Still, north of the line, or south of it, it remained the land that had been bought by the "blood, groans and tears" of many men, dark-skinned as well as white. And the events of the future would show how many remembered that—and cared.

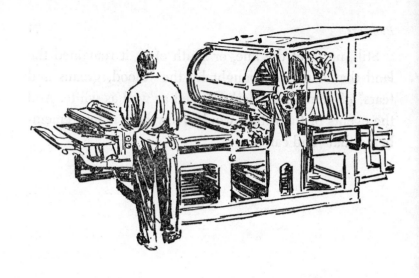

8 *Spokesmen*
1820-1832

There was a great bustle everywhere, of growing and building. The Erie Canal was under construction, a canal that would run all the way from the upper waters of the Hudson in New York to Lake Erie in the West. The steamship, once considered the greatest of follies, was growing more and more popular. Dozens were being built in the waterfront cities. Dozens were steaming along the broad rivers of the East and the South, making regular trips up and down the Ohio River and the Mississippi.

In the North, more and more small factories, iron

foundries, cotton mills, woolen mills, slaughter houses meat-packing houses, and lumber mills were being built. Settlements were springing up along all the rivers.

In the South, the big plantation owners were building fine houses, extending their holdings, and perfecting their lavish, gracious way of life. Less fortunate southerners, with little or no land or slaves, dreamed more than ever of how fine it would be to live in the same way.

And north and south, a new clamor was arising that all men should have a share in running the country which they were helping to build. People wrote and argued that all men should have the vote, whether they owned property or not. Only when every man could vote would America become a real democracy.

They meant all *white* men. Even in the North, most laborers clamoring for the vote ignored the Americans of African ancestry who were also furnishing the strength that was building the country.

Here and there, Negroes of talent, intelligence and persistence seized on what few opportunities there were, to speak out for the people of their race.

A truly unusual opportunity came to a young man named John Russwurm. Son of a white father and a West Indian mother, he was allowed, in spite of his dark skin, to enroll in Bowdoin College, in Brunswick, Maine.

His fellow-students at Bowdoin included several young men whose names would one day become well-known— Henry Wadsworth Longfellow, Nathaniel Hawthorne, Franklin Pierce, and Calvin Stowe, who would be best-known as the husband of Harriet Beecher.

Young Russwurm's eagerness to speak out against slavery in the South and the lot of all American Negroes was so great that even before he was graduated he joined with a friend, Samuel Cornish, to publish a small newspaper—the *Journal of Freedom*. It was the first Negro newspaper in the United States.

But not many people were interested in the message of the paper. Russwurm grew more and more discouraged. He was graduated from Bowdoin College in 1828, the first young man of Negro blood to graduate from a college in the United States. John Chavis, a generation before, had been privately tutored at Princeton.

A college degree seemed an empty honor, however, if no one listened to what a Negro American said or wrote. John Russwurm began to agree with the idea of the Colonization Society, that emigration to Africa was the only hope for Negroes. He felt, he said, that it was "a mere waste of words to talk of ever enjoying citizenship" in America.

His friend, Samuel Cornish, disagreed with him, and was determined to continue the newspaper. But soon Russwurm made up his mind and sailed for Liberia. Before too many years, he would become supervisor of schools in that country.

The bustle and the clamor went on. Russwurm's departure left no ripple. Cornish's newspaper, which he was still stubbornly publishing, hardly made a ripple either.

North, south, east and west, people were excited about the election. The laboring men, the workers, the men without property *had* been heard. In many states, they had won the right to vote. And Andrew Jackson, "the people's President," had been elected.

Rich men, men of property, bankers, merchants, lawyers, ministers were somewhat frightened. They foresaw a rule of the mob. But cheers went up from workingmen everywhere. America was becoming a real democracy for everyone. Except for the Negroes.

David Walker was an intense, intelligent young man who had had one small advantage. He was born in the South, but his mother was a free woman. And since, in the South, children had the same status as their mothers, David was free also. As a free Negro, he had traveled through many southern states before making his way north to Boston. There he went into business, managing a secondhand clothing store.

But what he had seen of slavery in the South had burned itself into his mind. He had struggled to educate himself, but he had seen hundreds and hundreds of Negroes, kept so ignorant by their owners, and southern laws, that they did not know enough to *know* they were uneducated. He saw how that kind of ignorance became a vicious circle. Uneducated parents, without ambition, or even any ideas of how things might be different for their children, could only raise children more ignorant and hopeless than themselves.

David Walker began to write a book. He wrote about everything that had shocked him. And he attacked the people of America who allowed or tolerated slavery while still professing to follow the Christian belief in the brotherhood of man.

A few people did notice and read what David Walker had to say when his book, *An Appeal to the Colored Citizens of the World, and Particularly Those of the United States,* was published, in 1829. Chiefly, they noticed and read because they were alarmed and horrified. They did not want Negroes to become aware of the way they were being treated and used in America. They wanted them ignorant—and obedient.

Just nine years before, another plot for a Negro revolt had been uncovered in Charleston, South Carolina. The white men of the South were still alarmed at how nearly this revolt, led by a free Negro named Denmark Vesey, had come to succeeding. When copies of David Walker's *Appeal* appeared in the South, the white men who read the book became frightened. Various southern governors put a price on Walker's head—ten thousand dollars if he were taken alive, a thousand if he were taken dead. One governor wrote to the mayor of Boston about Walker's book, asking that it be banned. The mayor replied that he did not like it either, but was not able to ban it by law.

Then, the brief excitement caused by the book was

over. A year later, David Walker died, still a very young man. Whether it was a natural death, or had been plotted, or if he simply died of despair, no one knew, or seemed to care.

The books people really liked to read in these bustling, busy years were books that praised America or told of its glorious past.

Washington Irving, genial, humorous and sentimental, had long since won a wide audience for his stories about the old days when New York had been the Dutch colony of New Amsterdam. Both in America and in Europe, people enjoyed reading about the thrifty, prosperous and superstitious Dutch burghers in New Amsterdam, or on their rich farms along the Hudson River.

James Fenimore Cooper was also winning fame with his exciting, adventurous tales of the days when upper New York State had still been a wilderness. Cooper wrote of the resourcefulness and daring of the early frontier scouts, and of the nobility and loyalty of some Indians— and the cruelty and treachery of others.

Then Cooper began writing books more critical of America, criticizing the rough, careless, destructive ways of the pioneer settlers who followed the scouts. And his popularity vanished. People were angered by that sort of writing. Those pioneer settlers hacking down forests, building shacks and barns and stores and mills, whom

Cooper criticized, were the new democracy. What did it matter if many of them were uneducated, loud and unmannered? They were building up the country, people said proudly, making themselves and the country rich.

Those two determined Negro leaders in Philadelphia, Richard Allen and Absalom Jones, decided that if Negro Americans united in some fashion, perhaps their voices might be more clearly heard over all the clamor and bustle of the white men's activity.

There had never been any real organization of Negroes in America, except in church groups. Wherever slavery existed, such organization had been made impossible by the slave owners. And even when slavery had ended in the North, most Negroes there thought of themselves first as Americans, eager to prove themselves among other Americans, and hardly interested in setting themselves apart as a special group.

But now Allen and Jones organized a convention of free colored people to meet and discuss what might be done to make Negro voices heard, and to improve the situation of Negroes everywhere.

The convention met in 1830, and though few except those at the convention listened to what was said there, a start had been made. Those conventions of Negro Americans, united in a common cause, would continue, year after year, growing larger each year. Finally, the men

and women who attended them would be able to add
their united strength to the efforts of a few white men
and women who *were* beginning to speak out in behalf
of the Negroes of America.

Those few men and women were having almost as difficult a time being hard as the Negroes themselves. It was
curious, in a way, for these were years when white men
and women all over America were eagerly discussing all
sorts of farfetched plans for reforming America and
making it even more wonderful than it was.

Some of them planned to establish towns or settlements
where no one would own property individually, but all
would share equally in the products of the work of all.
Some of them thought everything would be better if
young people were taught more trades in school, carpentering, brickmaking, all kinds of manual labor, instead of
so much Latin and Greek. Some of them believed that life
would be perfect if everyone's diet were changed and no
one ate bread that had been raised with yeast. Some were
interested in spiritualism. Some thought magnetism could
cure all diseases. And some thought that the bumps on
peoples' heads could explain their characters.

Nobody was outraged by any of these ideas. Many
were curious, interested, and then convinced by one or
all of them.

It was only when somebody suggested that America

would be a better democracy if slavery were abolished in the South and Negroes everywhere treated as citizens that almost everybody else banded together to try to silence the speaker.

A few persisted in preaching that reform, even so. A lawyer in Alabama, James G. Birney, freed all the slaves he had inherited, and then left his home, first to lecture against slavery, and then to start a newspaper dedicated to its abolition. He was driven out of one town after another, but he would not give up.

Two rich businessmen in New York, the Tappan brothers, were wealthy enough to ignore the anger that was aroused by their stand against slavery. And they donated sums of their money, year after year, to help anyone who was speaking out in that cause.

One day, one of the brothers, Arthur Tappan, received an urgent note from Baltimore, Maryland. A young newspaperman he knew was in jail there, for having started an antislavery newspaper. Would Mr. Tappan put up the bail?

Mr. Tappan did put up the bail. The young newspaperman, William Lloyd Garrison, was freed, and left Baltimore for Boston. In Boston, again with help from the Tappan brothers, and a few other people who shared their sentiments, young Garrison started another newspaper to preach against slavery.

Garrison called his paper *The Liberator,* and in the first issue, which came out early in 1831, he wrote, "I am in earnest; I will not equivocate; I will not excuse; I will not retreat a single inch; and I WILL BE HEARD."

"I will be heard!" He set it in bold type to show how much he meant it. But could he be—above all the clamor and bustle, the building, the growing, the planning of Utopias, and the studying of magnetism and head bumps?

White men in the South, growing more and more sensitive to any criticism of slavery, saw copies of Garrison's paper. They reacted just as they had to Walker's *Appeal.* They put a price on Garrison's head, and wrote to Boston, asking that *The Liberator* be suppressed. They seemed to have no trouble suppressing books and magazines that were unfavorable to slavery in the South, and thought northerners should not have any either. But once again, the mayor of Boston did not see how he could take legal action in such a case. Instead, various people in Boston simply tried to make things so unpleasant for Garrison that he would give up the paper.

But Garrison would not give up. Week after week, he put out his paper, attacking slavery, attacking slave owners, attacking everyone who allowed slavery to continue by paying no attention to it.

Not long after Garrison's paper was started, a slave in Virginia, named Nat Turner, rallied a band of Negroes for a revolt. His desperate group managed to kill more than sixty white people before they were caught. Almost hysterical with fear, the white people of Virginia—white people all over the South—blamed Garrison's writings for having inspired the Negroes to that kind of rebellion.

It was most unlikely that this was true. Long before Garrison started his paper, Nat Turner had been reading the Bible and finding his inspiration for revolt in the story of the children of Israel, held in bondage by the Egyptians.

But throughout the South, slave owners and poor white farmers became more opposed to letting Negroes learn to read. They tightened all the laws regulating the lives of slaves even more. Patrols were formed, to ride the roads and woods and check on any Negroes who seemed to be away from their assigned labors. Often enough, these patrollers were poor white men who owned no slaves themselves, but took pleasure in being people of importance in this way.

Still Garrison kept on putting out his paper. And here and there in the North, other men started similar papers. James Birney began publishing a newspaper called *The Emancipator* in Cincinnati, Ohio. He was attacked by mobs which often included some of the so-called best citizens of the city. Elijah P. Lovejoy, publishing an anti-slavery paper in Illinois, had his presses wrecked three times. Then Lovejoy himself was killed by a mob.

This kind of violence finally began rousing many northerners from their indifference to the problem of slavery.

Almost all of them were shocked that Lovejoy should have been killed simply for saying that slavery was wrong in a democracy. More and more people began listening to Garrison, to Birney, and to the others who were also speaking out.

Enough people had been aroused by 1832 to organize a New England Anti-Slavery Society. It was enlarged into an American Anti-Slavery Society the next year, with branches in towns and cities across the North. Dedicated to the abolition of slavery in the United States, the men and women in these groups now shared the same goals as the Negro men and women who had begun meeting in annual conventions in 1830.

And now, at last, as white Americans and dark began speaking out together, they would be heard.

9 *Artists, Writers—*
and Runaways
1832-1860

"Turn about an' wheel about an' do jis so
   An' ebery time I turn about I jump Jim Crow."

The song was just one of many lively tunes that were part of those crude, cheerful entertainments known as minstrel shows. White actors, their faces blackened with burnt cork and wearing grotesque clothes, capered, danced, sang, told jokes and put on skits. And traveling up and down the country in troupes, they brought gaiety and rhythm to people whose lives were generally hard, dull and without other entertainment of any kind.

They also brought inspiration to one musical young man in Pittsburgh, who later worked for a while in Cincinnati and watched the minstrels who came to that city also. He began to write songs of his own for the minstrels to sing—gay songs, foolish songs, and sad and wistful ones too.

Soon, with the minstrels singing the songs in one town after another, people all across America, even those who never went to minstrel shows, were singing "Oh, Susanna," "Nelly Was a Lady," "Camptown Races," "Old Black Joe," and many more of the young man's songs.

In the inspiration they gave to Stephen Foster, the minstrel shows were responsible for some of America's best-loved melodies. But the shows had one result that was not so fortunate. They gave many white people the idea that real life Negro Americans really resembled the burlesqued black men that the minstrels portrayed on the stage. Even people who knew Negroes who were quite different from the blacked-up stage characters, began to believe that Negroes in general were lazy, foolish, fond of watermelon and long words that they did not understand.

It was a curious time for such an idea to become popular. There were many more talented Negro Americans expressing themselves in writing, in painting, and in other creative ways than there ever had been before.

In New Orleans, especially, where free "men of color" had always known unusual opportunities and privileges, it was a time of a real flowering of the arts.

Many young men of this free group in New Orleans were sent to France for their education. Victor Séjour, very gifted as a poet, had enjoyed university years in France. Returning to New Orleans, he applied himself seriously to his poetry.

Camille Thierry, educated by tutors, was another young New Orleans poet. He and Séjour collected some of their best poems, and also a few by other young poets of the city, and had the collection published in a small volume called *Les Cenelles*. This book was the first anthology of Negro poetry in America.

But the young men, more European than American in their education, wrote their poems in French, which limited their audience.

Séjour continued to write. Inspired by stories of the brave Negro regiments with Andrew Jackson in the War of 1812, he wrote a long verse drama celebrating their exploits.

But no special attention or recognition was given to this work either. Finally, Victor Séjour decided to leave America to live in France permanently. In France, Alexander Dumas, who was part Negro, was one of the most popular novelists of the day. No one thought about his color there. In France, Victor Séjour also found recognition, and became a popular and successful playwright.

Soon Camille Thierry also left America and settled in France to spend the rest of his life there.

Edmund Dédè was another talented man who began his life in New Orleans. Musically gifted, he studied the violin and became a brilliant player, and an accomplished composer, as well. He too had to go to France before his talents were recognized. There he became the conductor of a symphony orchestra. Two brothers, Lucien and Sidney Lambert, were concert pianists. They found success touring Europe and South America.

There were Negro painters and sculptors in New Orleans also. Julien Hudson painted many of the distinguished men of the city and state, and two of his portraits still hang in the Cabildo in New Orleans. Two more brothers, Eugene and Daniel Warburg were sculptors.

New Orleans also produced an inventor during these years. Norbert Rillieux, like so many of the other young men, went to school in France. Then he stayed on as a professor. But along with his teaching, he began experimenting with the processes by which sugar was extracted from sugar cane. Before long, he had invented a new kind of evaporating pan for the sugar syrup, a vacuum pan that greatly speeded up the sugar-making process.

Rillieux's experiences after that were in happy contrast to those of the poets and musicians who had to leave America to find success. It was only when Rillieux returned to America that he was able to interest some sugar manufacturers in his invention. Later, after Louisiana sugar makers had put his invention to use and found it successful, French manufacturers also began to adopt it.

But New Orleans was not the only place in America where talented Negroes were appearing.

A boy destined to become America's first great tragic actor grew up in Maryland. His name was Ira Frederick Aldridge, and his moment of opportunity came when the famous English actor, Edmund Kean, appeared in Baltimore during the course of an American tour. Young Aldridge was hired by Kean as a valet and dresser. Kean soon became aware of the young man's dramatic talents and began coaching him. On his return to England, he took Aldridge with him, and continued the coaching.

Soon Aldridge was appearing in minor roles, and then came the night when he starred as the Moor in Shakespeare's *Othello*. He won an ovation for his performance in that role. Then he went on to almost equal success in other Shakespearean roles. He traveled to the continent and appeared in Paris, Brussels, Berlin, Rome, and finally in Russia, winning acclaim everywhere.

At last, Aldridge decided on a tour of his native land and came back to America. But in America he found audiences small. Few people seemed interested in seeing a Negro *tragedian*. Accustomed as they were to minstrel show comedians, they hardly believed that a Negro could play serious and powerful roles.

And so Aldridge went back to the continent, where he remained an honored and famous star for the rest of his life.

But the story of the Negroes in America was not all a story of talented people leaving the country in disappointment and despair during these years.

A new kind of hero was appearing on the scene. And with the help and encouragement of the men and women of the antislavery societies, these new heroes—and heroines—were becoming known as few artists and writers were.

They were men, and women too, who had accomplished the most dramatic and meaningful feat that there was for Negroes in a land of slavery. They had run away from slavery to freedom.

Negroes had been running away from their so-called owners, of course, ever since the first days of slavery. But these were the years when more and more white northerners were determined to aid them. Some aided through that system known as the Underground Railway, sheltering runaways secretly in their homes, and then helping them on their way toward the North, and the homes of more sympathetic men and women, until finally, the runaways had reached the free states, or Canada, which was safest of all.

Other sympathetic northerners helped the fugitives to get started in a new life, in the North. And then, one and all, the fugitives were encouraged to tell their stories to the world. For the antislavery workers were convinced that when men, women and children who had really known and endured slavery told their own experiences of what it was like, then the northerners who were still indifferent to slavery would have to listen and be roused to action.

Running away was in itself an act of fearful daring and courage. Southerners were watching all the Negroes among them more carefully than ever, and inflicting terrible punishments on any who were caught and suspected of running away. But once a runaway was safely in the North, it took almost as much courage all over again to stand up and publicly announce what he had done and who he was. Slave owners were determined to track down and seize runaways whenever possible, and take them back to the South. They hired slave hunters whose only job was just such a hunting down of runaways. And they offered large rewards for information from anybody that might lead to a slave's return.

Still, in spite of the difficulties that lay in the way of escape, thousands of Negroes did get to the North in these years. And of these thousands, there were hundreds who were willing to dare even more, and admit it.

There was the man, soon known as Henry "Box" Brown, who had himself nailed up in a box and shipped by railroad, steamboat, and wagon express to the North.

There was a woman, Ellen Crofts, light in color, who disguised herself as a white gentleman. Pretending that her darker husband, William, was her slave, she and he traveled openly on the dusty southern roads that led northward.

There was a young mother who, with her baby in her arms, took advantage of a cold winter that had frozen the Ohio River from shore to shore. She crossed that dividing line between the slave states and the free on foot —over the ice.

There was a man, much trusted by his owner, and allowed to travel freely, who wrestled in his conscience between his duty to his master, and his own right to be free. Finally, he decided the argument by taking off for Canada one day. After he had safely arrived there, he became a minister, helped other fugitives, and wrote a book about his experiences.

The young mother, known only as Eliza, and the trusted slave, whose name was Josiah Henson, would one day be the inspiration for two characters in Harriet Beecher Stowe's *Uncle Tom's Cabin,* a book that would sweep the whole country, rousing northerners to an awareness of the evils of slavery as nothing else had done.

But before that, there would be more runaways, many more. One little boy was taken north by his fleeing parents. Then his parents were seized by slave hunters and returned to the South. The boy, Henry Garnett, was rescued and befriended by antislavery workers, who sent him to school. Later, he became a powerful speaker at antislavery meetings and congresses.

A young man, William Wells Brown, born into slavery in Kentucky, was hired out by his owner to work on the river boats. Again and again, he tried to escape and failed. Finally, he succeeded and made his way to Canada. There he worked on Lake Erie steamboats, helped other runaways, and wrote the story of his experiences into a book.

But *The Narrative of William Wells Brown*, published in 1847, was only the start of this man's literary career. A few years later, William Brown published a book of poetry, *The Anti-Slavery Harp*. Then he wrote a play, *The Escape*, which was produced in Boston in 1858, the first play writen by a Negro American to be produced in America. Later still, he would write a novel, *Clotel*, the first novel by a Negro American, and two histories of Negro accomplishments in America.

And there were others. Lunsford Lane, born into slavery in North Carolina, worked to buy his freedom from his owner, and then to buy freedom for his wife and children also. He knew such treachery from his owner, who kept raising the price for their purchase as soon as Lane had earned the sum agreed upon, that when Lane finally reached the North with his family, he too had a book to write, *The Narrative of Lunsford Lane*.

Lewis Clarke, a fair-skinned Negro who escaped disguised as a white man, also wrote a book, a *Narrative of the Sufferings of Lewis Clarke*.

James C. Pennington escaped not only to the North, but from the North overseas to Germany, where he attended the University of Heidelberg and earned a degree. His book, published in the 1840s, was *A History of the Colored People*.

Sometimes runaways who became well-known in freedom received letters from their former owners, offering to free them from the threat of slave hunters, if they would send their owners their purchase price. Some runaways, for safety's sake, paid the price.

But one young man, Jermain Loguen, answered fearlessly and scornfully when he received such a letter. He wrote back to the woman who had owned him and refused to pay a penny. Long ago, he said, he had vowed he would never pay for the freedom that was his birthright.

Freedom—the birthright of every American. More and more the runaways and their stories were forcing the white men and women of the North to think seriously about that American ideal. And then, finally, there were two runaways whose fame grew so great that there was almost no one, north or south, who had not heard of them.

One was a woman, Harriet Tubman. Not content with having escaped from slavery herself, she returned to the slave states again and again, to lead whole groups of Negroes along the route of the Underground Railway to the free states. Sometimes, when she was in the North, she would appear briefly at an antislavery meeting and speak a few words. But then she would be off again, to the South. And her achievements were more eloquent than any words. All told, she led more than three hundred people out of slavery.

The other great hero was Frederick Douglass, a self-educated man so intelligent, passionate and handsome that he towered like a symbol of what a brave, dark-skinned American could be. A wonderful orator, he converted hundreds to the antislavery cause by his speeches at meetings and church gatherings. And his book about his experiences both in slavery and freedom, *Narrative of the Life of Frederick Douglass,* was so well and dramatically written that it became the most popular and widely read of all the narratives by runaway slaves.

Freedom as a birthright. More and more, the most talented writers and poets of the North were speaking out on the theme. Ralph Waldo Emerson, the quiet, high-minded philosopher and essayist; John Greenleaf Whittier, the Quaker poet; William Cullen Bryant, poet and newspaperman—they were only a few of the many who were adding their voices to the chorus.

Meanwhile, the men of the South were growing angrier. Under the attacks of the antislavery people, they had stopped apologizing for slavery and insisting that it was necessary. They had begun to proclaim that the system of slavery was a positive good, for Negroes as well as whites, that Negroes were not fit for any other life than one of slavery, and that white men were doing them a kindness by protecting them in that kind of life.

They had begun insisting that every new state added to the Union should allow slavery and that wherever the American flag was raised, men should be permitted to own slaves as part of their American heritage.

Soon the slavery argument came to be involved with every new problem that faced Americans. The history books tell of laws that were passed, or not passed, as the men of the North and the South argued the evils or virtues of slavery.

The country's push to the West was also entangled in the slavery argument. Should Texas be slave or free? Then gold was discovered in California. And after the rush of men to that far territory had steadied down a bit, the men in California asked that the territory be admitted as a state—a free state.

There was an outcry all over the South. Many southerners were ready to leave the Union right then, if California were admitted without allowing slavery.

Then, once again, as so often before, there was a compromise. California was admitted as a free state, but in exchange, the men of the South had demanded a new federal law making it a crime to help or shelter runaway slaves.

The people of the North, aware of the courage and

daring of runaways as they had never been before, felt
that the Fugitive Slave Law was cruel beyond belief.
Many decided not to obey it.

The anger had hardly quieted, when a quarrel over the
Kansas-Nebraska Territory broke out. Should the states
formed of that territory be slave or free? Congress decided to let the settlers in the territory vote for themselves on the question. There was a rush of men to the
territory—some for slavery, some against, ready to fight
with guns for control of the elections.

It was then that a lanky Illinois lawyer, Abraham Lincoln, who had tried politics once before but given them
up, decided to run for office again. Everything he had
ever seen or known about slavery had turned him against
it. He said that if it were in his power to do so, he would
end slavery at once and forever. But he saw something
else too. He saw that the quarreling over the issue was
tearing the country apart. And he quoted the Bible: "A
house divided against itself cannot stand."

10 *War Heroes*
1860-1865

And so the war came, in spite of everything. And in both North and South, men declared it was a war for freedom. The southerners meant freedom for themselves—to leave the Union and preserve slavery. The northerners meant freedom for the slave, and no freedom for any state to leave the Union at will.

Just as they always had, in every war, Negro Americans rallied to help, although, plainly, in this war, it was the northern goal with which they sympathized. In various northern states, they formed themselves into companies and began drilling. Even in the South, where the white men tried to keep from their slaves any hint that their freedom might be at stake, there were many Negro Americans who sensed that freedom was the issue, and they waited and hoped for an opportunity to help the northern cause.

And then, just as in the Revolutionary War, Negroes were informed they would not be accepted in the army as soldiers. It was bewildering to those brave Negroes who had already dared so much for freedom. It was bewildering to all the white men and women who had worked so hard in the antislavery effort.

It grew even more bewildering as the war dragged on, month after month, with one Union setback after another, and President Lincoln saying nothing about it being a war to end slavery. He insisted that it was a war to save the Union. And he rebuked northern generals, invading southern territory, who declared, on their own responsibility, that the slaves in the territories they had won were free.

The abolitionists in the North were outraged. But the Negro Americans kept on drilling. And in whatever ways they could, they helped, convinced that an end to slavery was one of the goals of the war, whatever Lincoln said.

It was in the South, in the heart of Confederate territory, that a Negro seaman made one of the most dramatic contributions of all.

The sailor, Robert Smalls, was a crew member of the Confederate gunboat, the *Planter,* operating off the coast of South Carolina. Whenever the *Planter* was in its home port, the white captain and officers slept in their homes on shore, leaving only a Negro crew member on board to keep watch.

Smalls had thought about this arrangement for some time and made his plans. The night came when it was his turn to keep the watch and he was ready. He told his wife what to do.

Darkness fell, and his wife and children hurried secretly to the waterfront. A brother and his family, who were also part of the plan, joined them. Anxiously, looking all about them, they got into a small boat moored at the wharf. Smalls' brother dipped the oars as quietly as possible as he rowed the little boat past the Confederate ships anchored all around. He came to the *Planter.* Quietly, everyone in the little boat climbed aboard the gunboat and went below.

Just before dawn, Smalls fired the boilers and made ready to steam out from shore. He put on a coat and hat of the captain's that had been left aboard. Then he went on deck and hoisted the Confederate flag.

It was time to start.

The captain's hat pulled down around his ears, Smalls stood at the wheel, hoping that no one would be able to see much except his uniform in the dim light. He began steaming out of the harbor. Passing one ship after another, he gave the proper signal to each. And he steamed on—out, straight out, to the open sea and the rolling swells where the ships of the Union blockade were cruising back and forth.

Would someone aboard one of the ships in the harbor wonder why the *Planter* was taking off in such a dangerous direction? And follow?

Smalls steamed on. No ship followed. A Union ship showed dimly through the gloom. Smalls hurried to the mast, lowered the Confederate flag, and quickly hoisted a white flag of truce.

Then he went back to the wheel, to bring the *Planter* alongside the Union ship.

Wondering sailors looked over the side. And then when the captain of the Union ship had also appeared, Robert Smalls of South Carolina called out to him. He said that he was delivering the Confederate gunboat, the *Planter*, himself, and all his family to the Union forces, to use as they saw fit.

Everyone in the North was thrilled and delighted when news of Robert Smalls' daring action was published in the newspapers. Lincoln himself signed the order for Smalls to receive the reward money offered for any enemy ship. And Smalls became a pilot on a Union ship.

But still, the Negroes of the North were not asked to enlist.

And then, at last, Union forces managed to halt the Confederate forces striking northward through Maryland.

There was a Union victory at Antietam that gave Lincoln hope that the North might win the war after all.

Lincoln was ready at last to announce that the war did have something to do with slavery. He warned the men of the South that within three months all the Negroes in the states still in rebellion against the Union, would be declared free.

There was rejoicing among all those who had hoped so long for such an announcement. The rejoicing was even greater three months later, January 1, 1863, when Lincoln signed the Emancipation Proclamation, making it official. Huge jubilee meetings were held in various cities of the North. And the heroes and heroines of the long struggle against slavery, white-skinned and dark-skinned Americans together, were the centers of weeping, singing, applauding throngs.

Not long after that fateful day, it was agreed that Negroes would be accepted into the regular army. Frederick Douglass was asked to help recruit a regiment of Negroes in Massachusetts. Two of his sons were among the first to join the 54th Massachusetts Regiment. A hundred Negroes joined in Boston alone.

Taking command of the all-Negro regiment was a handsome, gallant young man, Robert Gould Shaw, a Harvard student and son of an old Boston family. He led the troops in a stirring parade through Boston as the new regiment started off on the first leg of its journey into action in the South.

William Lloyd Garrison stood on a balcony above the

line of march, his hand resting on a bust of John Brown, who had died for the Negro cause in Virginia before the war started. John Greenleaf Whittier, who had written so many poems against slavery, was watching too.

It seemed to them, as it seemed to everyone who was watching, that what so many had dreamed of and worked for so long was coming true. White and Negro Americans were fighting together for the country that both had helped to build.

With the 54th off to the battlefront, Frederick Douglass recruited another Negro regiment in Massachusetts, the 55th. The units of free Negroes who had been hopefully drilling since the beginning of the war were armed and sent into action. Other units were organized, the Kansas Colored Volunteers, regiments from Rhode Island. In Louisana, occupied now by Union forces, Negro regiments were recruited to fight with the northern army.

Then tragic news came to all those who had watched so proudly as the 54th Massachusetts paraded through Boston. Going into action for the first time, against Fort Wagner, outside Charleston, South Carolina, the regiment had met furious resistance. The men had fought gallantly, but more than half of them had been killed. Their young commander, Robert Gould Shaw, had also lost his life in the battle.

North and south, men and women were grieving for

sons, brothers, fathers, who were falling in battle. But somehow, in the North, there was something especially poignant about the destruction of this particular regiment that had symbolized so many hopes.

Then came news that was, in some ways, even more dismaying. After the first rush, Negroes were no longer hurrying to enlist in the Union Army. A regiment being formed in Pennsylvania could not attract enough volunteers to fill its quota.

Frederick Douglass, the man to whom everyone turned in any kind of crisis that involved Negro Americans, was asked to investigate. He found out that while white volunteers were paid $13 a month and furnished their clothes, Negroes were paid only $10 and had to furnish their own clothes. Enlistment bounties and promises of advancement were given to whites but not to Negroes. Worst of all, Negroes taken prisoner by the Confederates were not treated as prisoners of war, but either put into slavery or sentenced to death.

It was the same old story that had threaded through the years, of *some* white men, even those fighting in the cause of freedom, refusing to grant that Negroes were Americans like themselves, deserving exactly the same rights as they accepted the same responsibilities.

Frederick Douglass went directly to Lincoln with the grievances. The President was distressed, and promised that the southern treatment of Negro prisoners would be promptly protested. He said he would gladly sign every recommendation for advancement that was presented to him. And he promised to do what he could about the other complaints as well.

After that, Douglass was able to offer Lincoln's own promises of better treatment, and Negro enlistments began to increase. Soon Negroes were serving in every field of action, as soldiers, sailors, spies and scouts. Lincoln was true to his word about offering them advancement in rank, too. Before the war was over, more than seventy-five of them would be commissioned as officers.

The history books tell of a million and a half men serving in the Union Army during the Civil War. They do not always add that 186,000 of these soldiers, or almost one-eighth of the total, were Negro Americans. They tell of 360,000 Union soldiers dead—killed in battle, or dying from wounds. They do not always add that 38,000 of these were Negro Americans.

Gettysburg and Vicksburg were the great battles of the summer of 1863, the great Union victories. Then came Chickamauga, Chattanooga, the Wilderness—the history books have a roll call of all the battles in which brave men of the North and the South, brave men both white and dark, fought and died.

And now, as the northern forces marched farther and farther into the cotton country of the deep South, hundreds of Negro field hands, whose masters and overseers had gone to war, were leaving their cabins to throng after the soldiers. Singing, dancing, clapping, they were joyful at the simple fact of freedom alone.

But ragged, penniless, untrained for any task except chopping cotton—how were all these refugees to live? Unable to read, to write, or even to imagine where their next meals were coming from if not provided by their masters, how were they to take care of themselves? They could not go on forever, trailing along with the army, confusing discipline and maneuvers, causing havoc at mess time, sleeping in the fields and roads at night.

There were people in the North who had realized a problem like this would arise. There were many who knew that for all the hundreds of intelligent, capable Negro Americans who had had a few opportunities and made the most of them, there were thousands and thousands of Negroes in the South who had never had any opportunities at all to become self-supporting.

Camps to feed and shelter the freedmen who had left their homes were set up behind the Union Army lines as quickly as possible, and wherever possible. Soldiers marching southward tried to direct the singing, rejoicing freedmen back to these camps and sent them off toward them, through the ravaged land of the South.

Education was going to be almost as important as food and shelter to these freedmen. And many in the North had realized that also. Almost as soon as the war started, Freedmen's Schools had been set up behind the army lines, in shacks, in tents, in cabins. Men, and women too, as dedicated as any soldiers or nurses, had traveled from their homes all over the North to teach in these schools.

The camps were soon crowded. So were the schools. Supplies were often delayed in a land at war, and no one knew what would happen on the morrow.

Still the volunteers in the camps and schools did their best. And still the refugees from farther south straggled in. Some of them had known so little of any world but the fields that they wore no shoes, did not know how to eat off plates, and hardly knew how to speak English. And still no one working to help them gave up hope. These men, women and young people from the fields would learn, as human beings had always learned, given an opportunity.

And still the Union armies held their gains in the South, in spite of all the desperate southern attempts to drive them back.

Sherman was besieging Atlanta. Then Sherman was marching from Atlanta to the sea, cutting the Confederacy in half.

Then, finally, the next spring, the Union's General Grant was hammering again at the Confederacy's General Robert E. Lee, in Virginia. Lee's forces were exhausted, hungry, almost at the end of their endurance. Lee was planning one of his swift, beautifully timed retreats. Then the retreat was cut off by Union forces. On

April 9, 1865, Lee surrendered to Grant at Appomattox Court House. The war was over.

For the southern states it was time to give up their dream of being free in a confederacy of their own. Defeated in battle, it was time to acknowledge once again that they were part of one family, the Union. And as members of the Union, they had also to accept the fact that in their states, as in the northern ones, no people could be held as slaves.

The Union had been preserved, and all Americans everywhere in that Union were free.

11 *Senators and Lawmakers*
1865-1877

The first Negro American to serve in the Senate of the
United States was Hiram Rhodes Revels. He was appointed in 1870, by the Mississippi legislature, to fill out
the unexpired term of Jefferson Davis, who had left the
Senate in 1861, to be President of the Confederacy.

After Revels' term had expired, another Negro American, Blanche K. Bruce, was elected by the voters of Mississippi for a full six-year term in the Senate, and he
served there from 1874 until 1880.

These were days and years of pride for Negro Americans everywhere, as one after the other, two dark-skinned men served with quiet intelligence in the highest law-making assembly in the land. They were also years of satisfaction for white Americans who had always believed that the color of a person's skin had no bearing on his or her abilities.

There were even more Negroes in the House of Representatives. Jefferson Long of Georgia was the first to take a seat in the House in 1870. Later, Robert Smalls, who had daringly steered the Confederate gunboat, the *Planter,* into Union hands, was elected to a seat in the House from his home state, South Carolina. In the ten years following the war, five more Negro Americans were elected from South Carolina and eight others from other southern states.

All of these men served with honor and dignity, just as Revels and Bruce did in the Senate. All of them members of a race that had long been mistreated in America, they might have been excused for spending most of their time trying to pass laws favorable to Negro Americans. But they did not do that. They were concerned, of course, with laws that would give equal rights to Negroes, but they were Americans first of all, dealing with every sort of problem that naturally came up before the Senate and the House, problems of national defense, national improvement, and international matters.

With such men serving in the national government, and other Negroes serving for the first time in state and local governments, it could have been a time almost as exciting and promising as the years after the Revolution when the white men of America first tried to prove that the system of democracy could work.

But it was also a time when many white men in the South, still unhappy about their defeat in the war, did not see the situation as promising and exciting at all. To them, it simply seemed that the victorious men of the North had arranged things so that they, the white southerners, would be humiliated and punished by having Negroes in positions of authority over them.

These southerners, when they began reorganizing their state governments after the war, had not planned to give any Negroes the right to vote. Instead, they passed laws that restricted the freedmen almost as harshly as they had been as slaves. They were granted the right to go to school, if Negro schools were available. They were required to work at some kind of job. And that was about all.

Northerners were outraged when they discovered that this was how southerners planned to treat the Negroes whom the Union armies had fought so long to free. One group of Republicans, members of the party that had elected Lincoln, was so extreme in its feelings, that it determined to teach the vanquished southerners a lesson.

Lincoln was dead, Lincoln, who had hoped to bind the nation together again "with malice toward none and charity to all." The extreme Republicans, called the Radical Republicans, were in control of the Senate and the House, and along with their sincere desire to improve conditions for Negroes in the South, they also felt a great deal of malice toward white southerners. They determined to raise one at the expense of the other.

Laws were rushed through that denied the right to vote to any white southerner who had taken any part in the rebellion or held any office in the Confederacy. At the same time, the right *to* vote was given to every Negro freedman, regardless of his qualifications. Then the senators voted to send Federal troops and military governors to the South to enforce these new laws.

The world seemed turned upside down to the white men of the South. The aristocrats and cavaliers who had ruled the big plantations, who had been the governors, judges and lawmakers of the South, were altogether without power. Even the poorest white southerners, who had always been able to tell themselves they were better than Negroes, did not have a vote if they had fought in the war. The ex-slaves did.

Hundreds of unscrupulous northerners hurried to the South to try to take advantage of the new power of the ignorant, uneducated ex-slaves. The least honorable of the southern white men, the ones who had fled from any service in the war and tried only to make money during those hard years, also had the vote. And they too hurried to make the most of the situation, using the votes of the ex-slaves to put themselves into office.

Horrified by the activity of all these greedy, selfish

men, most white southerners were completely blinded
to the fact that *some* of the Negroes among them were
educated, talented men. They were blinded to the fact
that even when the northern "carpetbaggers," and the
southern "scallywags," and the ex-slaves combined forces
in an election, they did not elect so many Negroes to office, in spite of their opportunity. And when they did
elect Negroes, they semed, by some instinct, to select
those well-qualified for office.

The white southerners saw only that they were without power, and that many men whom they had been
trained to think of as inferior to themselves held that
power.

And so, when Hiram Revels first appeared in Washington, D. C. to take his seat in the Senate, it was weeks
before the other southern senators would admit him to
the assembly. Revels was an educated man who had
never been a slave. He had been a minister in the northern states, then principal of a school in Baltimore before
moving to Mississippi. But the white senators from the
South tried to keep him out of the Senate by claiming
that he had not been a United States citizen for nine
years, as Senate rules required, because Negroes in Mississippi had not been counted citizens that long.

Later, when Blanche K. Bruce appeared at the doors
of the Senate chamber, he waited, as the custom was,
for the senior senator from his state to come and greet
him and escort him to the rostrum to be sworn in. The

white senior senator from Mississippi remained in his seat, refusing to recognize the waiting senator-elect. Finally, a senator from New York ended the embarrassment everyone was beginning to feel by going to greet Bruce himself, and escorting him to the rostrum.

Bruce was also a man of intelligence and refinement. He had been a slave, but a fortunate one, educated along with the young son of his master. Later, the son had taken Bruce with him to the war. But Bruce had not been able to endure playing any role in the Confederate cause. He ran away, traveled in the Middle West, taught school, studied at Oberlin College, and then, finally returned to Mississippi after the war. There he became a landowner and cotton planter.

But none of these qualifications, none of these achievements mattered to most white southerners.

A new kind of warfare had begun in the South, a one-sided warfare of the white man against the dark one. White southerners who had lost their right to vote began using all kinds of tactics to keep the Negroes who had won that right from using it. They threatened Negroes, frightened them and beat them. They discovered they could play on the superstitions of ignorant Negroes by riding the night in white sheets and hoods. An organization called the Ku Klux Klan was born of this discovery, and dedicated to frightening Negroes so badly that they would not dare to use their new rights as citizens.

In Louisiana, in South Carolina, in Mississippi, Negroes had become assistant governors. There were some Negro Americans in most of the southern state legislatures. Most of them were faced by the challenge of writing new constitutions for their states. By and large, the legislators, both white and dark, were serious and responsible about this. They passed many laws for public education and the general welfare that were so sensible they were retained through the years.

There was some graft and misuse of public funds in the southern legislatures. There was a great deal of that everywhere, in the Senate and House of the United States even more than in the state assemblies. But no Negro American in Congress was ever involved in any such activity. And even in the southern states, it was most often the southern "scallywags," or northern "carpetbaggers," who were guilty of using public funds for their own benefit.

But every scandal, every evidence of graft, was blamed on the Negroes by many white southerners. And gradually, by riding the nights in white sheets, by threatening, by withholding credit and withholding jobs, the white men were beginning to win back a sort of undercover control in state after state.

Then came the election of 1876, when it looked for a time as if the Republican, Rutherford B. Hayes, had lost to the Democratic candidate, Samuel Tilden, the first Democrat even to come near victory in years. There was consternation among the Republicans who had been in power so long. Then they realized that if two doubtful southern states switched their electoral votes to Hayes, Hayes would be the winner.

No one ever knew for sure if the Republicans made some sort of deal with those southern states. But history books tell of how those southern states did switch their votes to Hayes. And then they tell of how, once Hayes had become President, all the Federal troops and military governors were removed from the South, and restrictions that had been placed on white voters were lifted.

The white men of the South were free at last to openly take over control of their state governments. They were free to write into law all sorts of qualifications and amendments that made it very difficult for Negroes to vote. Before long, they had almost cancelled out the provisions of citizenship that had been given to Negro Americans after the war in the Thirteenth, Fourteenth and Fifteenth Amendments of the Constitution.

The years known in the history books as the Reconstruction Era were over. The South was not really reconstructed to the same rich land it had been. Fine homes and lavish plantations had not been rebuilt to the same glory they once had known. Money was scarce. People were in debt. The veterans of the war who had come home tired, ill or wounded, were still tired, crippled men, unable to take command of things in their old, aristocratic way. A new kind of man, the businessman, was coming into power.

A few more Negroes would be elected to the House

of Representatives in Washington, from districts in the South where the white men still had not managed to take the vote away from Negroes completely. Some of them, like John Mercer Langston, of Virginia, professor of law at Howard University, were brilliant men.

Presidents of the United States would continue to appoint outstanding Negroes to various official posts. Frederick Douglass, the grand old man of the Negro race till the day of his death in 1895, would be the trailblazer in many of these offices, first as United States Marshall, then as Recorder of Deeds for the District of Columbia, and finally as U.S. Minister to Haiti.

Ex-senator Bruce would follow Douglass as Recorder of Deeds. Other Negroes would be sent on diplomatic missions to Haiti, Liberia, and the Dominican Republic.

Negroes were also becoming teachers, professors, and scientists in various schools and colleges both north and south. They were becoming ministers of influence, doctors, dentists, newspapermen, businessmen. The time had long since passed when one could count in a paragraph or two the Negro Americans of achievement, emerging from a blurred mass of people in slavery.

Still, the white men of the South, their land unreconstructed in so many ways, were well on their way to reconstructing one thing that had existed before the war —a world where all opportunities were denied to men and women whose skin was a different color from theirs.

12 *Laborers, and Others*
1877-1896

Never had there been so many worlds in America, a land that had always held many varied lives.

There was the world of the wealthy—a world of palatial homes, shining carriages, glittering jewels, brilliant balls and tours of Europe.

There was the world of the poor, huddled in slums and tenements just around the corner from the rich world. Never had there been such a tide of immigrants—over five million coming in one year alone. These immigrants faced many of the same problems that Negroes had faced a hundred, and two hundred years before. They had to learn a new language, new ways of doing things, and in most cases, only their labor was valuable. They had just one advantage over the Negro Americans who had met and struggled with the problems before them. The color of their skins did not cause other white men to deny them opportunities to advance, once they had shown intelligence and initiative.

There was the world of industry, a world of smoking factories, of mills, mines and railroads, where most of the new immigrants found a market for their labors.

There was the world being created by a host of new inventions—Alexander Graham Bell's telephone, Thomas Alva Edison's brilliant experiments with electricity. Soon Edison's electric light would be illuminating homes, factories and buildings everywhere. The typewriter, the cash register, the linotype machine were transforming offices, stores and newspapers. And new machines were speeding up processes in every sort of factory.

A few clever Negro Americans were playing their part in that world of invention. Jan Matzeliger, who had been born in Dutch Guiana, came to America as a boy and went to work in a shoe factory in Lynn, Massachusetts. As people with creative minds have always done, he did more than just learn to use the machinery. He studied it and thought about it.

He pondered on one final step in the making of shoes that was still done by hand. Then he began experimenting and kept on until he had invented a machine to take care of that final handicraft process. The machine did its work so well that the United States Shoe Company bought the invention from Matzeliger. After putting it into use, the company cut its cost for making shoes by 50 per cent.

John P. Parker was another Negro inventor, who devised a new sort of screw for tobacco presses, then established a foundry company and made presses for many businesses. Elijah McCoy, still another Negro American, grew interested in how engines and machines might be oiled without stopping their motors. He finally patented fifty different automatic devices which solved this problem for as many different kinds of engines.

Electricity, steam boilers and air brakes interested Granville T. Woods, and several of his inventions were purchased and put to use by large industrial firms.

There was a world of art and music and literature, also. Mark Twain was writing his tales of life on the Mississippi and introducing Americans to two unforgettable boys, Tom Sawyer and Huck Finn.

A southern writer, Joel Chandler Harris, had also created an unforgettable character, Uncle Remus, who retold all the old tales and legends with which Negro slaves had amused themselves in the days before the war —tales and legends that Harris had heard and loved in his childhood.

There were also Negro writers, making use of the same

kind of American fantasy and folklore. Charles W. Chestnutt was the most famous of these. Chestnutt had been
born in North Carolina, and lived there until he was a
young man. Then he went north, to Cleveland, Ohio,
and studied first to be a legal stenographer, then for the
law. But all the while, in his spare time, he wrote stories
about some of the people he had known in the South—
uneducated but shrewd, superstitious but wise, oppressed
but full of laughter and humor.

When Chestnutt began to sell his stories to the *Atlantic
Monthly*, few of the readers who admired them had any
idea their author was a Negro. They were simply caught
up in the spell Chestnutt wove, living in the world he
created.

Soon Chestnutt was able to give up the law and devote
himself entirely to writing. He published his collected
stories in a book called *The Conjure Woman*. Then he
went on to write novels, *The House Behind the Cedars*,
The Marrow of Tradition, and *The Colonel's Dream*, all
of them thoughtful, dramatic and beautifully written.

Other Negro Americans were writing books of history
and biography that focused on the achievements and adventures of dark-skinned men and women in America.

A Civil War veteran, George Washington Williams,
spent years of research on a long, thoughtful *History of
the Negro Race in America from 1619 to 1880*. Scholars
everywhere admired the book. Later, he wrote a *History
of the Negro Troops in the Rebellion* which became the
classic work on that subject.

The first Negro American ever to attend West Point

Academy and receive a commission from that school, Henry Ossian Flipper, wrote a book about his experiences as *The Colored Cadet at West Point.*

A Negro woman writer, Sarah Bradford, wrote a biography of Harriet Tubman, *Harriet, the Moses of Her People.* Frederick Douglass brought his autobiography up to date.

There were Negro poets during these years as well. Albery A. Whitman, James Madison Bell (who had been a friend of John Brown), Frances E. W. Harper were just a few.

Edmonia Lewis was a talented sculptor. She studied in Rome and among her works were busts of John Brown, Lincoln, and others who had helped the cause of Negro freedom.

In the world of music, Negro Americans were also making names for themselves. Nellie Brown Mitchell, wife of one of the officers in Massachusetts' famed 55th Negro Regiment was a singer who became well known to white and Negro audiences alike.

A musical prodigy, "Blind Tom" Bethune, startled everyone who heard him. Born in slavery days, and blind from birth, he had been a child of four when it was discovered that he had a fantastic ear for music. After hearing a composition only once, he could play it note for note on the piano. As he grew older, he grew more and more accomplished. Even the most difficult works by Bach, Beethoven, Liszt only had to be played for him once, and he could repeat them.

After the war, the man who had previously been his

owner took him on tours all over the country, exploiting the blind pianist and keeping the profits of the concerts for himself. But no one who heard him could doubt that Thomas Green Bethune was a genius.

Six young women and five young men were also becoming well known, the best-known of all Negro American musicians. They called themselves the Fisk Jubilee Singers, for they were all students at a college that had been founded for Negroes soon after the war, Fisk College in Nashville, Tennessee.

They began singing as a group to try to earn a little money for a new building that was needed for the college. The songs they sang were the old spirituals and work songs from slavery years, which few white Americans knew in those days. Their first local appearances were so successful that they decided on a daring venture —a concert tour of various big cities in the North.

The northern tour was a triumph. After that, the Fisk Jubilee Singers went on to a tour of England, Germany and other European countries. And they knew even greater success abroad than they had known in America.

When they returned at last from all their tours, the Fisk Jubilee Singers had earned $150,000—more than enough to begin the building of a structure on the campus that would be known as Fisk Jubilee Hall. Perhaps even more important, Americans everywhere had now discovered a rich part of their musical heritage—songs like "Swing Low, Sweet Chariot" and "Go Down, Moses," which would never again be forgotten.

All kinds of worlds—worlds of music, of invention, of industry, and art—and Negro Americans were contributing to all of them.

There was the world of the West, also, where the ranchers grazed their cattle over vast plains, and cowboys rode the range, herding them, month after lonely month. There were Negro Americans among those cowboys, just as there were Irish and German and English Americans. All of them knew the same long hours in the saddle, the same hardships, the same wide, arching western skies, another world entirely from the world of the East.

And meantime, in the South, white men were trying as determinedly as possible to build still another world, where Negro men, women and children would remain in the same kind of helpless ignorance that the field hands before the war had known, and where only their labor in the field would be of any value.

It was to help the thousands and thousands of Negro Americans caught in this world that a man named Booker T. Washington devoted his life.

He had known the hardships and difficulties of this world himself, from the very beginning. Born just before the start of the Civil War, Booker could remember life in the rude cabin on the plantation, where his mother was a slave. He could remember the one rough flaxen shirt which was his only clothing, the rough, dirt floor

of the cabin, the meals with food snatched by fingers out
of the pot. He remembered, also, the end of the war, and
the owners in the big house summoning all the slaves
to tell them they were free.

After that, there had been years working in a salt mine
in West Virginia, with his step-father and brother, though
he was still only eight or nine. There had been his struggles to attend a small school for Negroes that was opened
in the neighborhood. Then he had learned as much as
the school could teach him, and his days were full of
nothing but work, serving as a houseboy to the wife of
the owner of the mines.

Then Booker heard about a school that trained Negroes
to be teachers. It was far away, in a town called Hampton, on the Virginia coast. But at last Booker had saved
enough to start out for this wonderful school, Hampton
Institute.

He bought a train ticket for part of the journey, but
then he decided to walk the rest of the way. Miles lay
ahead of him. Day after day, he trudged on. He came to
the city of Richmond, and no longer had any money for
food or shelter. He got a job working on the wharves till
he had enough to go on.

When he finally arrived at Hampton, penniless, tired
and dirty, he seemed a poor candidate for admission. The
woman in charge asked him to clean a nearby recitation
room. He was so anxious to do it well that he cleaned
it three times before he was satisfied.

Such eagerness could not be denied. Booker Washington was accepted as a student at Hampton, and it was arranged that he would help pay for his tuition by working as a janitor.

After he was graduated, Washington taught at Hampton for a while himself. Then came what seemed like his great opportunity—an offer to be the head of a new teacher training school that was just being established in the deep South, near Tuskegee, in Alabama.

Booker T. Washington met shock after shock when he arrived in Tuskegee. No building had been provided for the new school, nor were there any funds to build, buy or rent one. In general, the white people of the community did not want a school for Negroes nearby. Above all, Washington was dismayed by the lives of the Negroes who lived in this area.

A new system, called sharecropping, had been developed by southern landowners to take the place of slavery for working the land. And it had caught almost all Negroes in its toils. Families were given cabins, and a few acres of land to work. They paid rent for these by turning over a large share of the crops to the landowner each year.

The system worked very well for the landowners. Twenty years after the war was over, southern cotton growers were producing as much cotton as before the war. But the sharecroppers were not so fortunate. Bad years or good, the same amount of cotton was required by the landlord. Seeds, supplies, food, clothing, everything had to be purchased from the landlord, at any prices he chose to charge. Most sharecroppers were not only in debt, but going more deeply into debt every year.

Washington rode around the countryside, visiting the families of the district. They lived in rickety, windowless cabins. They did not grow anything but cotton, which they planted right up to the walls of the cabin. They ate nothing but grits and hogback, and such refinements as sitting down to a table set with knives and forks were unknown.

Washington *knew* about lives like these. Washington *knew* the kind of effort it took to work oneself out of such misery. It took effort like cleaning rooms, walking miles, working on wharves, working as a janitor.

He found a ramshackle church and got permission to hold his first classes there. He found two white men in Tuskegee who were sympathetic and helped him. He recruited boys and girls from the countryside to come and attend his school—bringing their own blankets and pots and pans.

Gradually, in spite of every obstacle, Washington's school began to take shape. It was part of his plan that the students themselves should do the building. Building a kitchen, a dining hall, a dormitory, they were not only creating a school, they were learning skills that would help them all their lives.

Not all Washington's students were pleased to find themselves hammering nails, laying bricks, spreading plaster. They had had cloudy dreams that going to school meant learning Greek and Latin and sitting in elegant ease. And when Washington set them to work in clay pits, digging clay to make bricks, they wondered what that work had to do with education.

But Washington persisted. He taught not only trades and skills, but such simple things as table manners, personal neatness, and the need for brushing teeth. And, of course, regular courses in English, mathematics, history and geography were part of the program too.

And gradually, the school began to grow, to flourish—to thrive. The white people around about began to look at Tuskegee Institute with more and more favor. The skills of the young people who graduated from it were very useful. Students began coming from all over Alabama, and then from nearby states also.

The fame of Tuskegee began spreading in the North. Washington took fund-raising trips there every year. He was a fine public speaker, and soon various northerners were contributing money to help Tuskegee continue and enlarge its services.

Gradually, white men of the South grew more and more pleased with Tuskegee, and with Booker T. Washington. In none of his efforts and activities was he interfering in any way with their own ideas that Negroes belonged in quite a different world than they did. He did not urge Negroes to be ambitious for the right to vote or to come into conflict with white people in any way.

His one goal seemed to be to teach them how to help

themselves to live useful lives, and to gain skills in jobs that needed doing. And for the particular people with whom he was working, it was indeed the goal that had to come before any other.

But the white men of the South now felt Washington's goal at Tuskegee was the proper goal for all Negroes everywhere. They saw him as setting an example for all Negroes. And finally, in 1895, they showed their approval in a most dramatic way. A great International Exposition was going to be held that summer in Atlanta, Georgia. The sponsors of the Exposition asked Booker T. Washington to make an address to the huge assembly of dignitaries that would be present for the opening ceremonies.

It was a time of triumph for Booker T. Washington. But also a time of terrible responsibility. He knew that if he offended the men who had so honored him, or made them feel that he was encouraging Negroes to have ambitions that the white men did not want them to have, they might easily find ways to end all his efforts at Tuskegee. Even the basic opportunities that were offered there might be denied to the thousands and thousands who had no other chance for education.

The opening day of the Exposition arrived. The throng gathered in the great hall. Then Booker T. Washington arose on the platform, dignified and self-possessed. He knew what he had to say.

He reminded the crowd before him that one-third of the population of the South was Negro, and that everyone's welfare was affected by the welfare of so large a group.

Perhaps, he said, in the first years of freedom, some Negroes had "tried to begin at the top instead of the bottom." (He was not the first Negro American to admit that after the Emancipation some freedmen had been more eager for the *look* of importance than an understanding of its responsibilities. Alexander Crummell, a brilliant minister and scholar in the North, had already spoken and written on the subject.)

But Washington continued. "It is at the bottom of life we must begin, and not at the top," he said. He addressed his fellow-Negro Americans with a parable, saying, "Cast down your bucket where you are," meaning that no task was too humble to do well.

Then Washington did his best to reassure the white men of the South that in seeking the opportunity to be good workmen and laborers, Negroes were not protesting any of the laws or customs that had been written or built up since the war by the white southerners.

"In all things that are purely social," Washington said, "we can be separate as the fingers, yet one as the hand in all things essential to mutual progress."

There was a tumult of cheering and applause when Washington finished. The dignitaries on the platform rushed to congratulate him. Reporters hurried to get the story of his speech on the wires so that it could be printed in papers all over the country.

Overnight, Washington became the most famous Negro in America, the man whom most white men were ready to accept as a spokesman for Negroes everywhere.

But not all Negroes everywhere agreed with all that Washington said. It seemed to them that in trying to protect the most basic opportunities for thousands of southern Negro Americans, Washington had had to ignore thousands of Negroes elsewhere who had long since left the ignorance of the cotton fields behind them.

And in saying, "we can be separate as the fingers," he seemed to be clearly approving all the new laws which kept Negro Americans from even the ordinary privileges of American citizens.

But all of that pleased most white men of the South very much, and many in the North as well.

13 *Partners*

1896-1910

Once again, Americans were joined together to fight a war. This time it was a war with Spain, triggered by the mysterious explosion of the American battleship, the *Maine*, in Havana harbor, off Cuba. Two hundred and sixty-six American officers and crew men were killed in that disaster, twenty-two of them Negro Americans.

The cry, "Remember the *Maine!*" echoed across America, and white men and Negroes alike rallied to the colors. Soon ships were steaming out of southern ports for Cuba, bearing troops, officers, chaplains and doctors, both white and Negro.

As it turned out, the war did not last long. And history books tell most often of the dashing young officer, Theodore Roosevelt, riding at the head of his Rough Riders to capture San Juan Hill in Cuba. The victory might not have occurred if it had not been for the efforts of the Negro soldiers of the Ninth and Tenth Cavalries, who rushed forward at a critical moment, knocking down a fort the Spaniards had improvised, cutting barbed wire, and making an opening for the Rough Riders.

Even before the attack on Cuba, American forces had also been attacking Spanish possessions in the Pacific. And Negro troops were also part of the victory in the Philippine Islands.

So a new century began, with the United States not only stretching from coast to coast in America, but holding island possessions in the oceans both east and west.

It was a proud time for some Americans, who liked the idea of empire. There were others, however, who were somewhat troubled by this kind of expansion. It seemed to them that America's swift years of growth had created many problems at home that should be solved before the nation went seeking for more territory.

The poverty of the thousands of immigrants from Europe disturbed these people. They were troubled by the hard working conditions in factories all over the country. Children were working in factories too, standing long hours at machines, never knowing school days, much less decent food, enough rest or time for play. Conditions in prisons were bad. Farmers faced special problems of their own.

Men like Jacob Riis and Lincoln Steffens began trying to arouse people in general to these miseries among them, with books, magazine articles and speeches.

Women like Jane Addams and Lillian Wald were founding settlement houses in slum areas, where children, and older people too, could gather for recreation, encouragement, even a little education.

Novelists like Stephen Crane, Jack London, Theodore Dreiser, and Frank Norris had begun dramatizing the various ills of American society in their books, picturing the hard lives of child workers, poor farmers, oppressed factory workers.

Somehow though, most of these dedicated reformers seemed to be blind to the plight of one group of Americans among them, who now made up a tenth of the population of the country, the Negro Americans.

"Separate but equal." That was the phrase the southern white men had invented in the days during and after the Reconstruction when they were trying to keep Negroes from any real place in their world. If the law required public education for all children, they would obey the law by providing education for Negro children as well as white—but it would be separate, in different buildings, in different parts of town. And they pretended these "separate schools" were equal in all ways to those provided for white children.

Libraries, where eager children could find books to read, hospitals for the sick, the injured of every age, were not covered by Federal laws. And so the white southerners shut Negro Americans out of their libraries and hospitals and said they might build their own libraries and hospitals, "separate and equal," if they wanted them.

Hundreds of small regulations and restrictions had been set up to separate Negro Americans from white Americans in all sorts of trivial ways. Negro women might cook for white Americans, raise their children, wash their clothes. Negro men might work side by side with white Americans. But Negroes had to ride in separate cars in the trains, separate seats in the busses, had to drink from separate drinking fountains, wait in separate waiting rooms, and if they wanted to buy a meal when away from home, or spend the night in a hotel, they had to find some "separate but equal" restaurant or hotel for Negroes alone.

"Jim Crow laws" these were called, from the old, old minstrel song, meaning, no doubt, that Negroes were supposed to "turn about an' wheel about an' do jis so" whenever white people told them to. They could live their lives in some "separate but equal" sort of way.

"Separate"—but very rarely equal. For when white men were dividing up tax money for schools, it seemed only logical to give the most of it to the schools which their own children attended. And when separate train coaches, separate waiting rooms, and so on were provided, there hardly seemed much need to make them "equal" for people who had no way of protesting. As for libraries and hospitals, it was naturally very difficult for Negroes who were pushed into the lowest-paying jobs to build any of those for themselves at all.

"Separate," but not equal at all. This was what had been written into law in the southern states, what Booker T. Washington had seemed to be approving with his famous speech in 1895—and what many people in the northern states were beginning to accept as the custom there too.

There were some white people—there had always been some—who realized how unfair this was, and what a handicap it put on some Americans who happened to have darker skins than others. There were church groups and philanthropists who contributed money through the years to help Negroes build up colleges and teacher training schools.

But somehow, the men and women so eager to reform America during these years spent little time wondering about what "separate but equal" really meant, nor why, granting accommodations and opportunities were equal, some Americans should be separate from the rest.

As always, since colonial days, some who were "separate" were making the most of what opportunities they had, with a genius that rose above "separateness."

A sensitive boy going to high school in Dayton, Ohio, showed such a feeling for words and the rhythms of poetry that his English teacher gave him all the encouragement she could and hoped that he might be able to go to college. But there was no money for that. After graduating from high school, the boy had to take a job running an elevator in an office building.

Still, his poems sang themselves in his mind as he drove the elevator up and down. In his spare moments, he wrote down the verses. When he had quite a few of them collected, he took some of the money he had saved from his salary of four dollars a week and had them printed in a small book. He sold the book to friends and to people who rode the elevator.

The poems in the book, *Oak and Ivy,* surprised and pleased the people who read them. Many of them were writen in the soft, slurred dialect of uneducated Negro Americans, and almost all of them told of everyday happenings—picnics, courtships, putting a baby to sleep. But they were full of rollicking rhythms and lively expressions.

> An' you couldn't he'p f'om dancin' ef yo' feet was boun'
> wif twine,
> When Angelina Johnson comes a-swingin' down de
> line.

The young poet began receiving encouragement from various people. Frederick Douglass, still alive in that year of 1893, helped the young man get a better job, at the

Chicago World's Fair. Then more and more white people began to take an interest in the poet's work.

When the young man had a second volume of poems ready, a regular publisher accepted the collection and published it. By the time he had a third book published, *Lyrics of a Lowly Life,* the career of a new poet had been launched. His name was Paul Laurence Dunbar.

Negro Americans everywhere loved Dunbar's poems, for he wrote of things they knew, and transformed the small joys and sorrows of life into songs. White Americans enjoyed them and admired them too. And Dunbar's life should have been happier now, for he was invited to teach and to lecture, and publishers were ready to publish anything he wrote.

But Dunbar was a poet who could sing as truly in the language of the great English lyricists as he could in dialect. He could write stanzas of quiet beauty which were universal in their appeal.

> Because I had loved so deeply,
> Because I had loved so long,
> God in his great compassion,
> Gave me the gift of song.

And yet Dunbar's poems that were written in serious and beautiful English were not popular. Neither were the novels he wrote.

He had never been very strong. The disappointment of never being recognized as a serious poet hurt him. All the thousands of small humiliations which Negro Ameri-

cans, as "separate but equal," suffered every day hurt
him also.

In the last stanza of his short poem, he wrote as though
he had failed as a poet.

> Because I have loved so vainly,
> And sung with such faltering breath,
> The Master in infinite mercy,
> Offers the boon of death.

And shortly thereafter, at the age of thirty-four, Paul
Dunbar was dead.

There were many, many Negro writers by now, men
skilled in newspaper and magazine writing too. Many of
them, accepting the banishment of "separate but equal,"
were establishing newspapers and magazines just for
Negroes, though their talents might have qualified them
for writing assignments anywhere.

There were many, many artists, painters and sculptors.
One who became especially distinguished was Henry
Ossawa Turner. Son of a Methodist Episcopal bishop in
Pittsburgh, Pennsylvania, Turner had been fortunate as
a young man. He had been able to study art at the Pennsylvania Academy of Fine Arts. Then, like many another
ambitious young American artist, he went to France to
study.

His talents grew and ripened in France. He began submitting canvases to various exhibitions and galleries. And

he began winning prizes, medals and blue ribbons. One of his paintings, a Biblical scene called the *Resurrection of Lazarus,* was purchased by the Luxembourg Museum and still hangs there.

Then Turner came home to America and began submitting his large, beautifully detailed religious paintings to exhibits and galleries. Again, his talent was recognized with first awards, medals and prizes. Still, the judges of one exhibition were so surprised to find that the first prize had gone to a Negro that they seemed about to withdraw the prize. It was only when some of Turner's fellow-artists gathered around him and walked up to the platform with him that the judges reconsidered, and gave him the medal he had won.

These were also the years when Negroes were first beginning to appear on the stage in America, in musical comedies and in vaudeville.

Bert Williams and George Walker were two of the first to show their talents as singers, dancers and comedians. However, white Americans were so used to the old minstrel show caricatures of blackfaced entertainers that Bert Williams had to blacken his face before going onstage, and both he and Walker had to change their normal speech to an uneducated drawl, before audiences would accept them as comedians.

Will Marion Cook had studied to be a serious musician, at Oberlin College, and then in Germany. But when he came back to America, he decided that a Negro violinist would have small opportunities there. He turned his talents to popular music.

Getting Paul Dunbar, the poet, to collaborate with him and write the lyrics for his songs, he wrote a musical comedy, *Clorindy*. It was the first Negro musical show ever to be presented on Broadway in New York, and was a great success. After that, Will Marion Cook went on to further successes in the musical comedy field.

Two brothers came north from Jacksonville, Florida, soon after the opening of *Clorindy*. Like the Gershwin brothers, who would become famous a generation later, one of them, J. Rosamund Johnson, was a composer, and the other, James Weldon Johnson, was a poet. They were still in Florida when they wrote a song that would soon become known to all Negro Americans, *Lift Ev'ry Voice And Sing*.

The Johnson brothers turned their talents to musical comedy also when they arrived in New York. *Shoofly Regiment* and *Red Moon* were just two of the popular shows they wrote.

They also wrote many songs together. *Under the Bamboo Tree* and *Oh, Didn't He Ramble* are still jazz classics.

J. Rosamund Johnson, the musician, continued to write for the stage, and for various singers. But his brother, James, began writing and publishing books of poetry. In *God's Trombones*, he recreated in poetry the excitement and drama of the sermons of the old-time preachers of the South, and the book was very popular.

Still later, James Johnson wrote a book that became a national sensation, *The Autobiography of an Ex-Colored Man.* He served in various governmental positions, one time as the American consul in Nicaragua, and worked to help the conditions of American Negroes in general.

A young man in Alabama with little formal musical training but a great gift for rhythm and melody was playing a cornet in a jazz band, much to the disappointment of his preacher-father. It was the beginning of a career that would one day make that particular musician known around the world as the "Father of the Blues," W. C. Handy.

A scientist, hired by Booker T. Washington to work and teach at Tuskegee Institute, was experimenting with some plants that grew very easily in the South—sweet potatoes and peanuts. Before long, George Washington Carver would be known all over the country for the dozens of products his creative imagination was able to devise from those two humble vegetables.

Other Negro scientists, doctors, scholars, lawyers and inventors, were contributing to the convenience and joy of life in America.

But in spite of all their accomplishments, the "separate" idea deprived them of the privileges of most Americans. And in the South, where white men had made a practice of terrorizing Negroes during the Reconstruction years, this kind of violent behavior was increasing.

A Negro had only to be suspected of some crime or infraction of the law and a group of white men was apt to seize him and hang him. More responsible and thoughtful white southerners might deplore these lynchings, but very few lynchers were ever punished. And so ignorant and brutal men engaged in the practice more and more freely. Soon there was an average of 160 lynchings a year in the South, or almost three a week.

And still, the plight of Negro Americans seemed of less concern to most reformers than the other miseries around them—child labor, slum conditions, long hours in factories.

Seventy-five years before, when the fortunes of Negro Americans had been at an even lower ebb, the two Philadelphians, Richard Allen and Absalom Jones had decided that Negroes had to unite and work together if their lives in America were to be improved. Now, in 1905, another troubled Negro American returned to the same idea.

William E. B. DuBois was a young man of extraordinary ability, who had had an unusually fortunate childhood. He had known happy high school years in Great Barrington, Massachusetts. He had gone to Fisk College in the South, and done so well there that he won a scholarship to Harvard University. After graduating with honors from Harvard, he had gone to Germany to study for two years. Then he had returned to America at about the time Booker T. Washington was making his famous speech in Atlanta, telling white Americans that Negroes should be content to begin at the bottom, and to be "separate as the fingers" of the hand.

Young DuBois had great respect for what Booker T. Washington had accomplished. He knew that the under-privileged Negroes of the South needed just the kind of training Washington was providing. But he could not approve of the way Washington seemed to accept the situation which deprived Negroes of citizenship. And he was alarmed at how many white Americans thought *all* Negroes should be limited to the simplest kind of education, fitting them only to be skilled workmen.

But DuBois had a scientist's mind. White Americans in general had a certain picture of Negroes, made up of minstrel show ideas and the behavior of field hands. He decided to make a careful study of a large group of Negroes to see if they were, in general, the way the white men pictured them.

Philadelphia, the home of so many outstanding Negroes of the past, was the city he decided to study. When he had finished, he had a five hundred-page volume on how the Negroes of that city lived and worked and played. Thoughtful scholars everywhere recognized the book, *The Philadelphia Negro*, as a work of great importance.

And what had it proved? That Negroes were a great deal the product of their environment, just as white men were, and that some Negroes, just as some white men, could rise above bad conditions, and some could not.

After that study, DuBois went on to write articles and essays for the *Atlantic Monthly*, and to teach at various colleges.

But all the while, conditions were growing worse for Negro Americans. And finally, in 1905, DuBois wrote to a large number of successful, accomplished men across the country and suggested that they meet to discuss what they could do to improve things.

The first meeting of this group was at Niagara Falls. An outline of aims was drawn up. Plans were made for another meeting. The next year the second meeting was held at Harpers Ferry, where John Brown had died for Negro freedom fifty-seven years before. More progress was made at the second meeting as the men exchanged views.

And then, that same year, there was a riot at election time in Atlanta, with white men attacking, beating and killing the Negroes of the city. Similar riots broke out in other cities. There was a fearful riot in Springfield, Illinois, when the white men seemed to go mad for a few hours and killed scores of Negroes.

Suddenly, the white reformers woke up. Perhaps it was the riot in Springfield, Abraham Lincoln's home and shrine, that shocked them the most. Nobody even knew what had started it. Stunned and horrified, the reformers realized that there was *one* evil in the country that was supposed to have been cured, fifty years and more ago, but had not been cured, after all.

Eighty years before, a white man, William Lloyd Garrison, had raised his voice against slavery and said, "I will be heard." Then white and dark Americans had begun working together and, uniting their efforts, they had helped to bring an end to slavery.

Now again, in 1909, white men and women realized it was time for white and Negro Americans to work together. A group of New Yorkers that included Mary White Ovington, a social worker, William English Walling, a writer on social reform, and Oswald Garrison Villard, a newspaperman and grandson of William Lloyd Garrison, sent out invitations to a number of white and Negro Americans to attend a national convention.

Jane Addams, Lillian Wald, John Dewey, Lincoln Steffens, and Rabbi Stephen S. Wise were just a few of the well-known white Americans who accepted.

William E. B. DuBois was there too, and so were the men who had joined him at the first convention at Niagara Falls in 1905.

At the convention, the first plans for a new organization were laid—the National Association for the Advancement of Colored People, generally called the NAACP. A few months later the society was formally organized and white and Negro officials were elected.

Full citizenship for Negro Americans was the society's one goal. The members of the NAACP planned to work for it by writing books, articles, lobbying in Congress, and above all, by taking legal action in all cases where Negroes were denied the rights of citizens of America. Dr. William E. B. DuBois left his professor's chair at Atlanta University to head the important department of publicity and research.

"All men are created equal . . ." A hundred and thirty-three years before, the delegates to the Third Continental Congress had first declared that great idea. Once again, the men and women who had worked together to build America were working together to bring that great idea a little closer to reality.

By Their Presence
Together ... 1963

Two hundred thousand men, women and children were
packed in the great esplanade before the Lincoln Monu-
ment in Washington, D.C. Many of them were Negro
Americans, but there were thousands of white Americans
with them. They had come from every part of the United
States to show, simply by their presence together in the
nation's capital, that all of them were still waiting for
Negroes everywhere to be given their full rights as citizens.

It was August 28, 1963. Two great wars had occurred
—and in both of them, Negroes by the thousands had
fought as bravely as they had always fought. There had
been a boom, a depression, a recovery.

There had been some progress too, in the granting of
citizenship to all Americans. The NAACP, through its

147

legal branch, had carried hundreds of cases involving Negroes' rights through the courts, many to the Supreme Court. Many of the restrictions that various states had put on Negro voting had been declared illegal.

Other organizations of Negro and white Americans had been formed, to work in their own ways towards the same goal as the NAACP. Groups had been founded to help Negroes who left farms in the country for the city, and found life there strange and difficult. Students, both white and dark, had banded together.

And much had been accomplished. Discrimination against Negroes on trains, busses and airplanes had been declared illegal. Segregation of Negroes in the armed forces had been ended.

Another even greater victory had been won. For years, dedicated lawyers, determined parents, and other concerned Americans, had been fighting case after case to prove that Negro children and young people, restricted to segregated schools, were not able to get the same quality of education as that provided for white children. At last, in 1953, the judges of the Supreme Court, by unanimous decision, declared that separate schools for white and Negro children *were* basically unequal, and hence against the law. After that, all American children were entitled by law to the same kind of education and preparation for their futures.

Along with this kind of progress, there had been other kinds of accomplishment. And the names—just the names alone—of Negro men and women of achievement would fill pages. In every field where white Americans were distinguishing themselves, there were Negro Americans doing the same. There were famous doctors, scientists, statesmen and lawyers. There were brilliant writers, poets, actors, actresses, singers and musicians. There were sports figures—baseball players, tennis players, track stars.

But still—in 1963—very few of these accomplished and acclaimed men and women could live their lives in America without, one time or another, being turned away from a restaurant, a hotel, even a hospital—because of the color of their skin.

And if it was still like that for even the most talented and fortunate, it was even more so for the millions who sought only an opportunity to go to schools where they could prepare for useful lives, or for decent jobs in fields where their interests lay, and where they could find opportunities to advance.

And in some states of the South, colleges and schools were still refusing to obey the Supreme Court order of 1953 to admit all qualified students.

The two hundred thousand men and women in Washington, D.C., in 1963 were there because a Civil Rights Bill, designed to end this kind of treatment of some Americans, was soon to go before Congress. They hoped to show, by their presence together, that the time had come for this kind of bill to be passed.

They met quietly, and they listened to the speakers.

Men who had become the leaders of Negro Americans in the last fifty years—ministers, lawyers, labor workers— spoke of their needs, their hopes and their rights. One leader, a minister, Dr. Martin Luther King, Jr., spoke of a dream also—a dream of an America where all the men and women who lived and worked there could live and work as equals.

Eleven months later, on July 2, 1964, the Civil Rights Bill, having been passed by both houses of Congress, was signed by the President and became the law.

There was still resistance among some of the white men in some of the southern states. Three hundred years and more of thinking that the color of their skin gave them some talent and ability denied to other men had left their mark.

But from the beginning, white men and Negroes had been together in America. Together they had made it strong.

And some day they might be able to make it the nation that most of them dreamed of—together.

A Few Suggestions for Further Reading

There are a number of fine biographies for young readers about Negro Americans of achievement who lived during the years covered by this book. Among them are:

Gould, Jean. *That Dunbar Boy*. New York: Dodd, Mead & Company, 1958.

Graham, Shirley. *Booker T. Washington*. New York: Julian Messner, Inc., 1955.

———. *Doctor George Washington Carver: Scientist*. New York: Julian Messner, Inc., 1944.

———. *Jean Baptiste Pointe De Sable: Founder of Chicago*. New York: Julian Messner, Inc., 1953.

———. *There Was Once a Slave: The Heroic Story of Frederick Douglass*. New York: Julian Messner, Inc., 1947.

———. *Your Most Humble Servant: The Story of Benjamin Banneker*. New York: Julian Messner, Inc., 1949.

Yates, Elizabeth. *Amos Fortune, Free Man*. New York: E. P. Dutton & Company, 1950.

There are also many individual biographies of famous Negro Americans of the twentieth century, and these too are available in the libraries.

Some interesting books that tell about many Negro Americans include:

Bontemps, Arna. *Story of the Negro,* 3rd edition. New York: Alfred A. Knopf, Inc., 1958.

Hughes, Langston. *Famous American Negroes.* New York: Dodd, Mead & Company, 1954.

———. *Famous Negro Heroes of America.* New York: Dodd, Mead & Company, 1958.

———. *First Book of Negroes.* New York: Franklin Watts, Inc., 1952.

Hughes, Langston and Meltzer, Milton. *A Pictorial History of the Negro in America.* New York: Crown Publishers, Inc., 1956.

Richardson, Ben Albert. *Great American Negroes.* New York: Thomas Y. Crowell Company, 1956.

Woodson, Carter G. and Wesley, Charles H. *Negro Makers of History.* Washington, D. C.: Associated Publishers, Inc., 1958.

A Selected Bibliography

These were the most helpful among the many books consulted to provide an authentic and balanced story of Negroes and whites in America.

Brawley, Benjamin. *The Negro Genius*. New York: Dodd, Mead & Company, 1937.

Bardolph, Richard. *The Negro Vanguard*. New York: Holt, Rinehart & Winston, Inc., 1959.

Bishop, Morris. *Odyssey of Cabeza de Vaca*. Watkins Glen, N. Y.: Century House, 1933.

Bontemps, Arna. *One Hundred Years of Negro Freedom*. New York: Dodd, Mead & Company, 1961.

Cable, George Washington. *The Negro Question*. New York: Doubleday & Company, Inc., 1958.

Douglass, Frederick. *The Life and Times of Frederick Douglass*. Riverside, N. J.: Collier Books, 1962.

DuBois, W. E. B. *Black Folk, Then and Now*. New York: Henry Holt & Company, Inc., 1939.

Franklin, John Hope. *From Slavery to Freedom: A History of American Negroes*. New York: Alfred A. Knopf, Inc., 1956.

Helper, Hinton Rowan and Fitzhugh, George. *Ante-Bellum: Three Classic Works on Slavery in the Old South*. Edited by Harvey Wish. New York: Capricorn Books, G. P. Putnam's Sons, 1960.

Hughes, Langston. *Fight for Freedom: The Story of the NAACP.* New York: W. W. Norton & Company, Inc., 1962.

Lomax, Louis E. *The Negro Revolt.* New York: Harper & Row, Publishers, Inc., 1962.

Myrdal, Gunnar. *An American Dilemma: The Negro Problem and Modern Democracy,* Twentieth Anniversary Edition. New York: Harper & Row, Publishers, Inc., 1962.

Olmsted, Frederick Law. *The Slave States, Before the Civil War.* New York: Capricorn Books, G. P. Putnam's Sons, 1959.

Redding, J. Saunders. *On Being Negro in America.* Indianapolis: The Bobbs-Merrill Company, 1951.

Washington, Booker T. *Up From Slavery.* New York: Bantam Books, 1963.

Wiggins, Lida Keck (Editor). *Life and Works of Paul Laurence Dunbar.* Naperville, Ill.: J. L. Nichols & Company, 1907.

Africa, an Historical Guide. Compiled by the faculty of P. S. 119, New York City, Beryle Banfield, Chairman, 1964.

The Negro in American History. Curriculum Bulletin 1964-65 Series, No. 4. Board of Education, City of New York, 1964.

Index

About the Author

In writing about America's history, Johanna Johnston is dealing with a subject of particular interest to her. In THOMAS JEFFERSON, HIS MANY TALENTS, winner of the Thomas Alva Edison Award in 1961, she painted a portrait for young people of that versatile eighteenth-century genius in terms of his activities aside from politics and statesmanship. An adult biography of Harriet Beecher Stowe, RUNAWAY TO HEAVEN, reflected life in America during the nineteenth century. In THE CHALLENGE AND THE ANSWER she was concerned with "words that shaped America's history" and recreated the historical background for over one hundred famous sayings and quotations from American history.

Miss Johnston has written books for very young children, too, among them SUGARPLUM, PENGUIN'S WAY, and the imaginative CLOSE YOUR EYES. Other biographies for young readers include THE STORY OF HANNIBAL and JOAN OF ARC, and for several years she wrote for radio, specializing in programs for children. One of her favorites was the popular "Let's Pretend" fairy-tale theater.

Johanna Johnston was born and educated in Chicago, Illinois, but now lives and works in New York City.